RHETORICAL TERMS AND CONCEPTS

A Contemporary Glossary

RHETORICAL TERMS AND CONCEPTS

A Contemporary Glossary

George Y. Trail

University of Houston

HARCOURT COLLEGE PUBLISHERS

Fort Worth Philadelphia San Diego New York Orlando Austin San Antonio
Toronto Montreal London Sydney Tokyo

Publisher	Earl McPeek
Acquisitions Editor	Julie McBurney
Market Strategist	John Meyers
Project Editor	Jon Davies
Art Director	Susan Journey
Production Manager	Angela Williams Urquhart

ISBN: 0-15-507236-6
Library of Congress Catalog Card Number: 99-60752

Address for Domestic Orders: Harcourt College Publishers, 6277 Sea Harbor Drive, Orlando, FL 32887-6777. 800-782-4479

Address for International Orders: International Customer Service, Harcourt, Inc., 6277 Sea Harbor Drive, Orlando, FL 32887-6777. 407-345-3800, (fax) 407-345-4060, (e-mail) hbintl@harcourtbrace.com

Address for Editorial Correspondence: Harcourt College Publishers, 301 Commerce Street, Suite 3700, Fort Worth, TX 76102.

Web Site Address: http://www.hbcollege.com

Harcourt College Publishers will provide complimentary supplements or supplement packages to those adopters qualified under our adoption policy. Please contact your sales representative to learn how you qualify. If as an adopter or potential user you receive supplements you do not need, please return them to your sales representative or send them to: Attn: Returns Department, Troy Warehouse, 465 South Lincoln Drive, Troy, MO 63379.

Printed in the United States of America

9 0 1 2 3 4 5 6 7 8 039 9 8 7 6 5 4 3 2 1

Harcourt College Publishers

PREFACE

Rhetorical Terms and Concepts: A Contemporary Glossary was developed originally as a teaching assistants' resource in a first-year second-semester college composition course and then produced for students in that course and in advanced composition. It has been used in English as a Second Language and critical-thinking classes, and, I have been told by former students, in practically all classes involving writing and as a resource for writing and reading argument in the world at large. In its earliest and in its present print iteration (as opposed to the photocopies for teaching assistants), it was written to be used by lower division undergraduates in universities, colleges, and community colleges, and it has been successfully used by several thousand of them. I must stress that it was not then and has not now been "simplified" or written "down" to that population. It has always been expected that the user will find a good dictionary helpful or, at points, even necessary. I have consciously tried to keep the glossary "small" (that is, portable, back-packable, carry-onable, purse- and jacket pocket–stowable), yet still offer the fullest development possible.

The glossary includes terms associated with basic philosophical positions (particularly those concerning the nature and constitution of the "real"), as well as terms which are usually thought to be descriptive of style rather than what is traditionally associated with the specifically "rhetorical." The nomenclature that has developed in philosophy as well as in literary criticism to describe ideas and to describe the forms of fiction and of poetry are almost uniformly useful in the description of how those ideas and those literary forms are used to influence opinion, are used, in short, to write argument. In the largest sense then this book offers a vocabulary of terms and concepts useful in describing and analyzing writing intended to persuade.

HOW TO USE THE GLOSSARY

This glossary has been developed as both a reference tool and as a stand-alone document that can be read, like an encyclopedia, by a user moving at random from entry to entry (or like an interactive computer text by a user pressing linked notations). Readers can also consult the concluding scan list of terms, which is provided more as a resource in which to look *for* a term than to look *up* a term. Alphabetically arranged texts don't need indexes.

For use in writing and critical-thinking courses, the glossary is, of course, intended as a supplemental rather than primary text. For the user who wishes to practice with the terms and concepts, there is also a Rhetoric/Reader called *Reading Writing: Argument, a Rhetoric and Reader* which is keyed to this book.

I would recommend that the beginning reader go through the text from ABSOLUTE to ZEUGMA at least once, being sure to read *each* entry but feeling free to follow the internal directions to "see also" whenever they occur.

I would also recommend that those using this book in a composition, rhetoric, or critical-thinking class be less concerned with distinctions among and between the terms than with associations among and between them. The "differences," for instance, between *metaphor* and *analogy* are slight to nonexistent in relation to the overarching concept that unifies them. Indeed, the more familiar the reader becomes with the concepts of rhetoric and rhetorical classification and designation the more the boundaries between the terms will fade and the more clearly the reader will see that it is not particularly appropriate to ask if a given passage in an argument is, say, an example of begging the question *or* of loaded diction. There is no reason why it can't be both and involve several other rhetorical devices as well. To try to isolate and specify any such differences is opposed to the basic intent of this document, which is to provide a series of terms and concepts integral to an understanding of the processes of rhetoric in order to enhance the abilities of the writer as analyst, consumer, and producer of argument.

Note that this is a *glossary* of rhetorical terms, not a *dictionary* of rhetorical terms. Dictionaries of rhetorical terms are available, and I particularly recommend Richard A. Lanham's *A Handlist of Rhetorical Terms*. Lanham's book is especially strong on classical designations for rhetorical "figures" and schemas of classification. This glossary is finally more concerned with concepts than with "names," per se. If the reader can accept the basic assumptions that what we call persuasive writing attempts to affect attitudes and actions, and that persuasive writing emerges from a deliberate series of choices made by a writer who wishes to produce that effect, then the rest is details. The analyst of rhetoric asks, and attempts to answer, the question "What was this writer trying to accomplish by presenting these specific words in this specific way?" The generator of rhetoric asks, "How can I write to best arrange and choose words to influence those whom I wish to convince of my point?" The more arguments we know, and the better we understand attempts at persuasion, the better we ought to be able to argue ourselves.

A REQUEST TO THE USER

I would like to stress that I have made no effort in this supplemental reference text to achieve an authorless and disembodied tone. This book was not written by a committee. It is my hope that the tone conveys to the reader that these definitions and discussions issue from a person, not an oracle, and from experience rather than contact with the Logos/Truth. I anticipate, indeed I hope for, resistance to some of the emphases of the text. Some of the entries are quite lengthy, and those constitute the central ideas around which the glossary is built. I further hope that readers/users will feel free to share their responses with me, and also share particularly apt examples of these terms and concepts. Unlike a speech, which has to be given, a piece of writing is always only at a stage of its development and can always be, and I hope will be, improved. I look forward to your transmissions.

gtrail@uh.edu

CONTENTS

INTRODUCTION

Rhetoric is a term of such wide application that it not only resists attempts to limit its meaning but also seems to constantly suggest new ones. I have adopted a very limited working definition to give the reader a comfortable place to stand while becoming more familiar with the terminology.

A subject at which one can become continuously more capable, rhetoric gives back almost exactly what is invested in it. As an aspect of language, it is constantly changing, so, as with language, we study it as a process rather than a field of fixed knowledge. And with this, as with any process, one can follow it, or study it, or participate in it, but never "master" it. (The term *master* itself is rhetorically and philosophically interesting in that its use as a verb is in many ways at odds with its use as a noun. In the latter usage, no one calls herself a master. Instead the title is employed by those who seek to study under an individual whom they recognize as particularly distinguished in a given area of endeavor. The master, or *sensei*, herself would not consider that area "mastered," but instead would consider herself a devoted student of it. See META-PHOR for further discussion.)

This glossary, then, cannot be considered as in any way definitive. Indeed, from its perspective the concept "definitive" itself is insupportable. This glossary is instead an introduction, an opening into what can, at its best, be a developing and lifelong relationship with the language, psychology, and methodologies of written persuasion.

For our purposes here, *rhetoric* will be initially defined as "the use of written language in an attempt to persuade." This definition differs from ways in which *rhetoric* is defined in other texts in two specifics: "written" language and an "attempt" to persuade. The terms may seem to need no further explanation, but they are important enough at the outset to elaborate on them.

Aristotle (fourth century BCE) is frequently held to have produced the earliest of what now amount to hundreds, if not thousands, of "rhetorics" ("how to" books dealing with persuasion). His *Rhetoric* sets itself out quite clearly as a guide for the orator, for the "public" speaker. In speech, whether that speech is delivered to a single person (as part of a conversation) or to a stadium full of people, there is present an element that all *written* argument lacks—immediate audience response. Writing, unlike speaking, is not a "live" activity. The writer cannot see her audience and can neither see nor hear its approval or resistance. She cannot know, or even in any crude way assume, that she has gained its "attention." Unlike a speaker, a writer cannot, in midstream, "adjust" her approach or emphasis or text to what seems to be meeting with the approval of *this* audience at *this* time. She cannot (college newspaper editorials to the contrary) write something like "SEX and DRUGS. OK, now that I've got your attention . . . " without making the silly assumption that the intended audience visually scans pages of text looking for titillating words. A *headline,* arguably, could interest a reader in *starting* to read an article, but no number of repetitions of the name of that reader's favorite leisure object of contemplation (fashion, basketball, copulation, urban renewal, Republican renovation, whatever) could *keep* her reading it. The reader's relationship to a written text is vastly different from an auditor's to a speech.

I hope that the reader can see here, for example, that when I move to point 2, I must do so without the assurance that I have made my first point clear–that the reader has understood my point 1–which I might have had were I lecturing on this subject. I move to the second point without affirmatively nodding heads, or pleased smiles. or that squint that indicates concentration and interest, which a speaker has to refer to. To sum up point 1, there is a significant difference between the ways that *written* attempts at persuasion take place and the ways that all and any *other* forms (radio or television speech, pictorial advertisement, committee meeting, etc.) of attempts at persuasion take place.

The Irish poet W. B. Yeats wrote that we make, out of our quarrel with ourselves, poetry, and out of our quarrel with others, rhetoric. One reading of what he means is that rhetoric is, and *must be*, public. It must assume an audience that, in one way or another, is "other." (This leads, often, to the mistaken assumption that arguments, discussions, "fields of persuasion," if we can so call them, are limited to two "sides," some sort of team association between "us" and "them." No subject, however, is so simple that there are only two positions that can be taken concerning it.) Because, then, of this complex and inexorable "otherness" of the target audience, all the rhetor can deal with as analyst or as generator of "persuasive" text are *attempts* at persuasion. As a teacher of rhetoric, and of the analysis of argument, I often see statements from students such as "This statement is convincing because the writer has presented evidence for it in the previous paragraph." Reinforcing this basic error, twentieth-century versions of post-Aristotelian "rhetorics" uniformly ask questions like "Why is the opening paragraph of X essay effective?" The reader may well find herself, personally, *not* having been positively influenced by the opening paragraph and having to practice the hypocrisy of looking back to find out what it was that the textbook writer was impressed with. We have here, in fact, a wonderful example of the tendency of pedagogy to beg the question (see BEGGING THE QUESTION). The "rhetorics" (textbooks that tell one how to win arguments) most often assume some ideal audience for a given argument. And they assume that that audience is "reasonable" and that it understands what amounts to "proof" and (mostly) why any *opposing* political/religious/ethnic/racial/gender group is likely to be "unreasonable" about whatever is the particular issue. The assumption is that there is some position that can be labeled "objective" (see OBJECTIVITY), from which position one can make appropriate decisions or, at least, recognize "logical" propositions.

The argument that this glossary will present is that "persuasion" is not a "fact" (see FACT). The statement "Any reasonable person would agree . . . " is a rhetorical gesture that begs the question of whether "reasonable" people could disagree and still think of themselves as "reasonable."

Whether a given piece of writing does or does not "persuade," in other words, is conditional upon, depends upon, *to whom and when and where* a particular attempt at persuasion occurs. What persuades me *today* may very well not persuade you (say, for instance, that the term *chairman* is inherently sexist). What persuades me today might not have persuaded me yesterday. If you will think back to an occasion when you became convinced of something you did not previously believe, I suggest that often you will find that what persuaded you was not the argument or the evidence *immediately* presented, but rather your willingness, for whatever reason, to be *receptive* to the argument. You may remember that an argument that persuaded you at the age of, say, eighteen, did not persuade you at fifteen or that an argument that persuaded you at twenty-five did not persuade you at eighteen. And if we can agree that a *written* argument is static, is frozen in a specific shape, then accounting for its being persuasive at one time and not at another must be attributable to a change in the reader, not the writing.

My own experience has been that two days or a week or even a year after I have rejected an argument I find myself in a discussion arguing *for* the position I had previously rejected. The argument stayed in my head, as it were, and convinced me while I wasn't paying attention to it. In computer terminology I was processing the argument in the background.

The novelist William Burroughs hypothesized that there could be an English sentence so effective that anyone who read it would die on the spot. Monty Python has a routine involving a joke so funny that anyone who hears it (or reads it) dies laughing. These examples are a commentary on "effectiveness" as a criterion for the judging of argument. The closer we examine the concepts involved, the more we are driven to affirm that although there are arguments that are more likely to be successful than others, there must be a number of given, specifically, that:

1) the arguer understands the positions held by those to be persuaded,

2) the arguer can make statements in support of her argument that are not in obvious conflict with principles held by those to be persuaded, and

3) the arguer can point out deficiencies in opposing positions that those holding the position would acknowledge.

To put it more briefly, we can say that *some* arguments are effective for *some* people *some times*. But we cannot ever answer the bald question "Is this argument effective?" without asking, "To whom?" and "Here?" and "Now?"

So, to sum up point 2, what I'm writing about, and what this glossary is meant to supply, is insight into how people use writing to *try* to persuade a particular group of other people at a particular time and in a particular place of a particular point—how people use writing to attempt to move a specific audience from one position in relationship to a particular issue to another position.

Nothing about the process is simple. Indeed, the process involves everything that is presently thought about human psychology and behavior. It involves logic. But logic is only one of its means of rhetorical appeal. It involves the invocation of deeply held beliefs, and it involves presenting and misrepresenting statistics. It involves appeals to racial pride, patriotism, and notions of "ethnic purity." It involves everything that we feel about anything that we think is important in and to our lives. Finally, it involves thinking about the bases of why it is that we think what we think.

GLOSSARY

ABSOLUTE

An absolute is a term such as *all, every, any, always, never, perfect, forever, everybody, nobody,* and so forth, that refers to all members of a given set and/or admits of no qualification. One should be alert when using absolutes because a single exception can call an entire argument into question. Absolutes, however, are often used as a form of emphasis rather than as argument, and when so used they indicate enthusiasm or a desire to preclude misinterpretation (or both) rather than faulty logic. Consider the rhetorical intentions behind the technically meaningless "longer than forever" and "better than perfect." Or consider the retort "*Everybody* knows that" to someone's question (for instance) "What's a 'foul shot'?" Assuming that the person asking the question is honest, she, for one, does not know what a foul shot is, so the absolute (*everybody*) in the reply is clearly in error. What is probably meant by the construction, however, is something like "*Everybody* who knows *anything* knows *that.*" That is, the statement is equivalent to the ("grammatically" nonsensical but perfectly clear) statement "You don't know nothing." The analyst should be very attentive to absolutes, particularly in terms of what the writer being analyzed hopes to accomplish with them. The analyst who encounters the phrase "all reasonable people agree" should be clear that this phrase is not an argument but rather an assertion that attempts to play on the reader's wish to be thought of as a member of the group "reasonable people."

An absolute is also a statement of fact or of principle that is held to be eternal and unchanging–as in the familiar phrase "absolute truth." Albert Einstein asserted that the speed of light is an absolute and that all other motion is *relative* to that absolute speed (see RELATIVE). This is the sort of meaning invoked when persons are asked if they are "absolutely" certain of something–that is, that they are convinced that *no* possibility of error exists.

ABSTRACT, ABSTRACTION

In rhetorical analysis think of "abstract" in relation to "concrete." It is George Orwell's "Politics and the English Language" that made these concepts into rhetorical principles. S. I. Hayakawa has contributed as well with what he calls the "Ladder of Abstraction." The higher one is on this "ladder," the less one can count on being clearly understood. (See LADDER OF ABSTRACTION.) As an example, consider Orwell's distinction between the phrases "elimination of unreliable elements" and "shot in the back of the neck." The first is abstract, the second concrete. Orwell says that abstract language is used in the "defense of the indefensible." For him it becomes a form of evasion, or a form of lying. It is used, and deliberately, when one *doesn't* want one's audience to see a picture, to imagine a "concrete" image. However, as Hayakawa's treatment makes clear, abstraction is essential to communication. The term *animals,* for instance, is an abstraction. There is no such "thing" as an animal at the concrete level–there is this goat, and this sheep, and this elephant, for instance, but there is no physical equivalent for the abstraction "animal." If, then, I want to talk about a subgroup of animals, like "pets," or even a subgroup of that group (say, "dogs"), I still have no choice but to be abstract. Otherwise I can talk only about a specific pet, who is probably a pet because he or she is in some way unique (or at least *I* think, like other pet owners, that my pet is unique).

Abstraction also refers to a *concept* that has no physical referent. Religion, courage, choice, and freedom, for instance, are abstractions, but they are not abstractions *of* a group of physically extant beings (such as the word *animal* is an abstraction of a group of physically extant beings). The concept of abstraction is extremely important in relationship to the idea of EXISTENTIAL IMPORT, and the discussion at that entry may clarify the foregoing.

Additionally, abstractions can be usefully considered in relationship to TROPES, especially given that the trope that has become existentially viable (say "animal") comes to be associated with particular characteristics and hence constitutes a metaphoric invocation of those characteristics. (Consider, for instance, what is "meant" when one person refers to another as "an animal.")

ACADEMIC ARGUMENT

To call an argument "academic," as to label an argument "rhetoric," constitutes an attempt to assign the discourse so labeled to a category somewhere outside of those modes of discourse that deal, supposedly, with "reality," or the "real world," or whatever word the categorizer chooses to label her own socioeconomic position. An "academic argument" in this sense is not an argument that deals with a subject in which people who live in the "real world" are seriously interested, although they might find the creations of the "intellectuals" interesting or some sort of curiosity. The argument labeled "academic," however, is, from this perspective, understood as only a waste of time, unlike the argument that is labeled "rhetoric," which is potentially dangerous.

When the term is used simply as descriptive rather than pejorative (usually from within "the academy," understood as an institution of higher learning), it describes a mode of discourse that historically precedes the ROGERIAN but closely resembles it. In its purest and most traditional form, the academic argument, so understood, argues a need for a question to be answered, reviews the literature on the subject to show that no answer heretofore presented is satisfactory, and formulates an answer that is submitted to the judgment of the academic community of the subject in question. The academic argument attempts to appear "reasonable" and modest rather than enthusiastic and proselytizing. Because Rogers's approach derives from his clinical experience, it is unlikely that the academic argument is its source.

ACCIDENT

In logic and philosophy (of which rhetoric is sometimes treated as a branch), the term *accident* is used in opposition to *essence*. It is of the "essence" of gold that it has a particular specific gravity and atomic weight. It is "accidental" that it is cast in the shape of a horse. Hence to say, "One must here distinguish essence from accident" is to say that one should not deny a given principle or idea on the basis of a particular instance of its use. The fallacy of accident is to argue from a general rule to a particular case, the "accidental" quality of which makes it an exception. Take, for instance, the general principle that "If one disobeys the law, one should suffer the penalties for so doing." A fourteen-year-old, finding a woman unconscious and bleeding to death in a farm yard, breaks the glass on the door of the farmhouse to find a telephone. Not finding a telephone she takes a set of car keys and drives the woman to the nearest emergency room in a car she finds parked in the farmhouse driveway. She is charged with breaking and entering, burglary, car theft, speeding, and driving without a license, under the general principle that does not take into account the circumstances (accident) that mitigate the principle.

ACCOMMODATION

To accommodate is to "create space for." Rhetorically the term refers to an attempt on a writer's part to include those with differing viewpoints or, more particularly, to avoid offending and thus excluding them. In general it shows respect for opposing viewpoints by including them in the discussion and admitting the soundness of aspects of them. ROGERIAN ARGUMENT builds accommodation into its structure. See TARGET AUDIENCE.

ACCOMMODATORS

Technically an *accommodator* would be "one who accommodates," but it here refers to words and phrases that are intended to signal that an aspect or aspects of an argument that lead to a disputed conclusion are being accepted as GIVENS or as TRUE. Frequently encountered accommodators are *given, granted that, it is true that, to be sure, it is certainly the case that, we will* [or *can*] *agree that,* and so forth.

ACRONYM   (*ACK* ROW NIM)

Acronyms can be represented in two distinct typographical modes. One of these notices the history of the formation of the acronym, and the other signals the acceptance of the construction as a word like any other. I can write, "WASP" (designating [w]hite [A]nglo [S]axon [P]rotestant), or I can simply write, "Your refusing to talk to her just because of that tattoo was really a Wasp thing to do." An acronym is any word formed of the initial letters of a series of words or an arrangement of the initial sounds of those words. They are pronounced in two ways, however. *NATO, UNICEF, NAFTA, snafu,* and *SWAT* are pronounced as they would be were they normal words. *G.I., F.B.I., USA, CD-ROM,* and *IBM,* which are equally acronyms, are pronounced one letter at a time. Note here that the first two acronyms in this series are printed with periods and no spaces following those periods, while the last three employ no periods or spaces. In post word-processing typography the tendency is increasingly to omit the periods altogether (*BCE, AT&T, PC,* etc.).

AD ABSURDUM   (ODD OBB *SURD* DUM; TO ABSURDITY OR FROM ABSURDITY; MOST FREQUENTLY SEEN AS "*REDUCTIO AD ABSURDUM*" OR EVEN SIMPLY "*REDUCTIO*"; RE *DOOSH* EE OO)
The *reductio* is a frequently used mode of argument that rhetorics often treat as a fallacy, although it is not. To apply a *reductio* to the argument that we should not eat meat because it (usually) involves taking the life of an animal and "all life is sacred," one would reply that human survival depends on the consumption of organic matter (i.e., matter that is either living or has been living). To be consistent with the "all life is sacred (and therefore should not be eaten)" argument, one would have to give up lettuce as well as hamburgers, the consequence of which would be that one order of "sacred life" (the human) would die out entirely and plants and other animals would go on unconscionably consuming one another.

AD BACULUM   (ODD *BAHK* YOU LUM; FROM POWER, FROM FORCE; LITERALLY, "FROM THE CLUB")

Although often so represented, technically speaking the *argumentum ad baculum* is not a fallacy in that it simply sets aside logical consideration in the face of consequences. The authority figure who finally replies, "Because I told you so" to an apparently unending series of "But why?" questions is arguing from force. This is not an appeal to authority (see AUTHORITY, ARGUMENT FROM, Latin classical *AD VERICUNDIUM*) because the authority has already been questioned; rather it says, "I will no longer argue—I have the power." In the game of poker, that three deuces and a revolver beat three queens is another example. See especially FEAR, APPEAL TO.

AD FEMINAM   (TO THE FEMALE)

The *ad feminam* argument resembles the *ad hominem* except that the attack on the arguer (as opposed to an attack on the argument) centers on the supposed "nature" of her gender. See GENDER and NATURE, ARGUMENT FROM.). The term, as here used, comes to us from the philosopher Jo Ellen Jacobs. At its most obvious level the *ad feminam* argument would involve, say, in response to the statement "That is a pretty patriarchal attitude," "Well, that's exactly what I would expect a woman to say." The point here, as in the *ad hominem,* is that the statement is true or false regardless of who makes it.

AD HOC   (ODD *HOCK* OR ADD *HOCK*, SOMETIMES ODD *HOKE*; "TO THIS")

An argument that is accused of being *ad hoc* is being labeled as a defense fabricated on the spot to suit the particular circumstances. The implication is that the argument is therefore inferior to other arguments with, presumably, more historical respectability. An *ad hoc* committee, from another perspective, is one that has a specific and limited charge or purpose, and the term here does not (usually) carry the pejorative associations of the *ad hoc* argument.

AD HOMINEM   (TO THE PERSON; USUALLY RENDERED AS "TO THE MAN")

This is an attack on the sayer rather than on the said. The truth of a given statement must, of course, be independent of who is stating it. (If it is true that Elvis Presley is dead, it makes no difference who says so.) When an attack on a position is personal as opposed to "factual," the question is whether the position at issue *depends* for its acceptability on the credibility of the speaker. If, for instance, a witness who is a known liar says, "I saw Sam shoot Bill," it is legitimate to question if the witness did or did not see this. However, the *statement* "Sam shot Bill" is true or false independently of who says it. Sam did or did not shoot Bill, no matter who says so.

An ENDORSEMENT is, in effect, the mirror image of the *ad hominem.*

AD HOMINEM CIRCUMSTANTIAL   (TO THE CIRCUMSTANCES)

This is similar to the preceding except that, instead of the person being attacked, the circumstances in which the statement was made are attacked or are used as reasons to discount the statement.

"GM is a great stock."
"Where did you hear that?"
"At a GM stockholders' meeting."
"Oh."

GM is or is not a great stock at any given time regardless of where or in what circumstances the statement was made.

AD MISERICORDIUM   (ODD MIS UR UH *COR* DEE UM; FROM
  PITY; LITERALLY, "FROM HEART PAIN")

The classic example of this appeal is the case of the attorney who argued that her client who had been found guilty of murdering her parents should be shown mercy by the court on the grounds that she was an orphan. This argument is related to *AD POPULUM* but is more specific in that it refers to only those commonly held values that *invoke pity*. Typically such appeals are to very particular circumstances and try to avoid involving related issues. See INDUCTIVE ARGUMENT.

AD POPULUM   (ODD *POP* YOU LUM; TO THE PEOPLE, TO THE
  GALLERY; BANDWAGON, "COMMON PRACTICE")

Such arguments attempt to link one subject to another subject that is held sacred or abhorred by the "masses"– such things in American culture as the flag, Mom, apple pie, baseball, freedom, and so forth, and conversely, communists, atheists, and homosexuals. Such associations are problematic on two grounds: (1) that such a link exists is *asserted* rather than argued (see ASSERTION) and (2) that a value is commonly held, or held by great numbers of people, is no evidence of its truth. One such *ad populum* argument that is seldom noted as such is the appeal to the greatness of the past. Often this is tied to the "the world is going to hell in a handbasket" argument (this isn't the way it used to be, so it must be bad).

AFFECTATION, AFFECTED

An affectation is a "put on" style. The person who is accused of being affected is being presented as being "unnatural" in the sense that she is thought to be behaving in a manner that is superior to her proper "place" in life. An affected writing style is one that is perceived as "fake" as the result of the writer using a particular choice of diction and sentence structure ("The reader, at this juncture, may well wish to pause and invest a moment in contemplation of the ephemera of quotidian existence . . . "). An American, for instance, could "affect" an upper-class British accent in an attempt to pass herself off as cultured. The analyst should note that a description of a writing style as affected assumes that there is a "natural" way to write, an apparently "everyday, matter-of-fact, ordinary" tone, which the analyst will recognize as representing a rhetorical choice on the part of the writer as much as would the use of any other tone. Thus a value judgment concerning the writer's ability may be less analytically useful than consideration of the possible rhetorical intention of the tone or the tone shift.

ALLUSION

To allude to something is to refer to it *indirectly,* and allusions vary greatly in how clearly they indirectly refer. Consequently it is seldom sufficient simply to assert that X is an allusion to Y–one usually has to present clear evidence to support such a claim. For example, it can be argued that the essay title "Of Whales and Wisdom" alludes to John Steinbeck's novel *Of Mice and Men* (four words, two of which are the same, and those that differ both begin with the same letter, as in the purported source) or that the essay title "Four-Letter Words Can Hurt You" alludes to the playground retort "Sticks and stones may break my bones, but names will never hurt me." P. J. O'Rourke titled one of his books *Give War a Chance,* alluding to John Lennon's "Give Peace a Chance." To say, however, "In this crisis, how far are we going to pursue the Moby Dick of parity?" is *not* to "allude" to Melville's whale, rather it is to directly *refer* to him.

AMBIGUITY

In rhetoric, as opposed to exposition, ambiguity, the capacity of being interpreted in more than one way, is, like the passive voice, a useful tool for attempting to prevent the potentially hostile reader from focusing early on a particular point of difficulty instead of reading further into the argument. This tool lends itself particularly well to the ROGERIAN ARGUMENT in which a basic strategy is to keep the reader involved until the point of the tentative conclusion. Ambiguity, in this sense, may be thought of as a sort of functional lack of clarity. If, for instance, I wanted to avoid immediately alienating an audience made up of people who consider homosexuality "unnatural" (which is in itself a highly ambiguous term), I might write about a "normal" distribution of the "components that fall within the range of what constitutes the sexually attractive" without any direct reference to same-sex attraction. Many more terms are ambiguous than might first appear, and here the analyst is referred directly to the entry for DEFINITION. It is important to remember, then, that the "ambiguous" is "unclear," in addition to being multiply interpretable. (One might say, for instance, that Tiger Woods's "race" or Mick Jagger's "sexual orientation" is "ambiguous.") Any term about which you could say, "It all depends on how you define it" may be thought of as "ambiguous." See EQUIVOCATION.

ANALOGY

To argue from analogy is to assert that what we already know of one set of circumstances can be seen as similar to another, and indeed similar enough that what has happened in one case can be assumed to happen in the other. Analogy is never PROOF and is instead judged according to its "strength." A strong analogy agrees in many points with what it is compared to, a weak analogy in a few or none.

Naturally, all analogy, if pursued far enough, will break down (on the simple basis that no one thing *is* another thing, and hence the comparison will at some point fail).

Perhaps the most famous analogy is the so-called "argument from design," which asserts that because natural things in the world appear to have some purpose, like something that *I* make has some purpose (ax, plow, whatever), it therefore follows that because *I* did not make the natural things in the world, some force much greater than I must have. Therefore God exists. Notice that this is *not* a proof, it is rather an *argument,* and its strength depends on the reader's estimate of the degree of correspondence between the things compared.

Beginning rhetorical analysts tend to refer to any analogy whose implications they do not like as a "false" analogy. This is a worthless designation for our purposes because, as earlier, *all* analogies are finally false, as *all* metaphors finally break down. To say an analogy is false, or even weak, is tantamount to saying, "This is not a persuasive analogy," which, of course, is unacceptable because it begs the question "To whom?" Analogies "work" or don't on the basis from which the audience receives them. Like metaphors they typically present a concrete image for an abstraction. If, for instance, I compare "the problem of poverty" to a water leak in a basement, I do so on the hope that the reader will find the image somehow apt. I can't *show* the reader "poverty" because poverty is a quality, not a "thing." I can give the reader examples of poor people, but poverty, in a sense, is what "contains" them and is not, in itself, visible. So to talk about poverty in any concrete way, I must either talk about specific instances of poverty or discuss it by analogy. See METAPHOR, of which analogy can be considered an elaborated or developed form.

Unlike analogy, which is intended to invoke points of similarity between two categories (one of which is usually abstract), negative analogy hopes to establish points of dissimilarity. Consider that there are two basic ways to describe a thing or a concept—one can say what it is like, and then what it is *not* like. This may be like the process that the mind goes through as it tries to identify and classify *any* unfamiliar object (or concept): the primary search is for an existing category into which an item or concept can be fitted, which search process necessarily entails the rejecting of some (or all) of them and thus recognizes *un*likeness or *dis*similarity. Thus it is valuable to know what a thing is *unlike* as well as what it is like. I began this paragraph with the word *unlike* in an attempt to both introduce the term *negative analogy* and simultaneously present an example of it. Negative analogy occurs in a wide number of common expressions, among which, in addition to *unlike* and *dissimilarly,* are *not to be confused with, as distinct from,* and the everyday *different from.*

Analogies and negative analogies often attempt to appeal to a reader on the basis of their wit, as in the bumper sticker that reads "A Woman without a Man Is Like a Fish without a Bicycle." The hope here, presumably, is that the reader may respond, "But what does a fish need with a bicycle?" and then on consideration see that that is exactly the point of the analogy.

ANALYSIS
As understood in "rhetorical analysis," analysis is the separation of a unit (speech, essay, paragraph, sentence) into its parts for the purpose of hypothesizing about the intended function of the parts in relationship to the whole. To analyze is not therefore to find fault with or to fix ("cure"). Analysis is often referred to in metaphoric terms as

"breaking down." "Breaking down" certainly has some negative associations, but "analysis," at least as it is being considered here, carries none of them. The expression "break it down for me" means "separate it into its constituent parts so I can see how it is intended to operate." One could also think of it in terms of an unfamiliar machine that one disassembles to see what makes it work. See RHETORICAL ANALYSIS.

ANAPHORA   (AN *AFF* OH RUH)
Anaphora, or repetition, is more frequent in speech than in writing, but it is found in writing that intends to approach the high ritual tone that might be described as elegiac or ceremonial (the "Gettysburg Address," for instance, a speech *designed* to be read, contains: "we cannot dedicate–we cannot consecrate–we cannot hallow–this ground").

ANECDOTE, ARGUMENT FROM
"Drug-related crime is completely out of control. On my way to the Senate today, I could see federal agents making a drug arrest in the park across the street from the White House itself." So might begin an argument in favor of increased spending for law enforcement or for a federal agency dealing with narcotics. An anecdote is a short narration of a "story" of an incident that is seen to be interesting, pathetic, cute, outrageous, illustrative, or funny. Most often the story constitutes a launch point for the argument to be presented and becomes a part of the evidence offered in support of the argument. That it is an anecdote distinguishes it from documented evidence of other sorts, so the form lends itself well to being crafted into a precise example of whatever point is to be argued. In that anecdotes are "off the record," are not "official" data, and hence difficult, if not to impossible to verify, they can be easily constructed

to perfectly fit the point. Often they draw their strength in an argument from the *ETHOS* of the writer–the perception that the writer is an honest person and so would not make up the story that she narrates as having recently occurred to her (and most often *very* recently–even on the same day, as an event that suggested that an argument needed to be presented in the first place). See INDUCTIVE ARGUMENT.

APERÇU (AA PER *SUE*)

The term would be used by an analyst in a structure such as "The writer here presents, as aperçu, that women, on the average, are shorter than men." That is to say, the comment is that the writer does not present her statement merely as an observation, but instead as if it were an insight, as if it were a particularly astute perception. "And then it came to me, *women are shorter than men.*" This example is deliberately unsubtle because what I mean to stress is that to describe a presentation as aperçu is to talk about the manner of presentation rather than to make a comment on the actual "insightfulness" of the comment itself. Like OBJECTIVITY, *aperçu* describes a rhetorical pose rather than confers a positive evaluation. See also EPIPHANY.

A second meaning of *aperçu* is as a name for a summary, outline, or synopsis.

APHORISM

An aphorism is a brief and usually easily remembered statement that asserts a value or a supposed "insight." An aphorism's attractiveness is probably to be attributed more to the cleverness of its expression than to the profundity of its content. Because an aphorism usually asks the reader to invest some work in decoding or figuring out its elliptical phrasing, the reader who "gets it" tends to be less critical of the content than if it were stated in a lengthy and ordinary way. Additionally, aphorisms are often felt to have "passed the test of time" and hence to contain "wisdom" that would, were it not accurate, have fallen out of the language. Here, technically, the appropriate term is *adage* or *saying* rather than *aphorism*. The authors of adages and sayings are "the folk," "anon.," or "traditional," whereas aphorisms, when quoted, pick up part of their cachet from the mention of the author's name, as in "time is money"–Benjamin Franklin (which then can be ironically replied to with "time is waste of money"–Oscar Wilde).

APHORISTIC
That statement that is described as "aphoristic" is brief, carefully worded, and presented as if it were a principle. See APHORISM.

APOLOGY
The "apology" and the "apologetic" are frequently employed rhetorical forms and can be considered as aspects of the tone described in the entry for MODESTY. In offering an apology or presenting something in an apologetic tone, the writer emphasizes to the reader that the reader is in the position of power in the relationship, that it is she who can accept or reject the apology. The appeal of such an approach probably lies in the notion that forgiveness is a virtue and that in granting it one becomes a better person. The reader has, in other words, an opportunity to feel better about herself and will associate some of the feeling with the writer who has asked for her forgiveness. She can say, in effect, "All right, I forgive you. Now what was it you wanted me to consider?" An ANECDOTE that the writer tells "on herself" is an often-invoked form of apology. In offering an apology for a particular statement or action, the

writer has a special opportunity to have the matter reflect as favorably as possible upon herself because she can define the terms and bring the rhetorical usage closer to the earlier use of the word, where it meant offering an explanation rather than expressing regret (John Henry Cardinal Newman's nineteenth-century *Apologia Pro Vita Sua* or Plato's "The Apology," Socrates' supposed statement immediately prior to his execution).

APORIA   (UH POUR *EYE* UH)

An aporia is a puzzling condition or situation. The rhetorical application of aporia is to pretend to an inability or confess to an actual inability to resolve a problem or answer a question. One might say of a political figure whom one was attacking, "I don't know what he lost first, his ability to tell the truth from a lie or his ability to behave morally." The device is often used when the question is being begged. A homely version of it is the often-heard comment "How can people be so stupid?" uttered when something the speaker disapproves of has just happened.

APOSIOPESIS   (APO SEEO *PEE* SIS)

Aposiopesis is much more common in speech than in writing, but in that writing that seeks the tone of the VERNACULAR it occurs frequently enough for the analyst to need a name for the practice. "In response to this, she said . . . , well, I think it would be better not to tell you what she said." The hoped-for effect is that the reader considers herself in a more immediate relation to the writer who is presenting thoughts as they occur rather than censoring them through the revised forms we are used to in writing (which would produce, instead of the previous sentence, something like "I won't repeat what she said in response to this").

The term can also refer to clearly implying an object or idea without specifically naming it. "In reply to what X suggests, I would say that had I known I was in a pasture when this argument started I would have been much more careful where I put my feet down." This second meaning for the term is another usage that is more frequent in speech than writing but that again, when it does appear in writing, often seeks the mood of the immediacy of speech.

APPROPRIATE   (UH *PRO* PREE ATE; VERB)

To appropriate something, as we might use the term in rhetoric, is to take an argument or a position from another, usually (although not necessarily) in a way that the other would not approve of. To appropriate, thus, is not to borrow (which involves the permission of the person borrowed from), rather it is to seize. It is argued, for instance, that so-called "right to life" advocates have "appropriated" the demonstration tactics of civil rights and antiwar activists. To use "appropriated" as a description of an activity in this way is intended to denigrate those supposedly doing the appropriation. One would not, for instance, say that civil rights demonstrators "appropriated" the methods of Gandhi because their activities would be seen as an extension of the principles behind Gandhi's efforts in India rather than in opposition to them. The use of the term thus constitutes LOADED DICTION in that it not only asserts "ownership" of a methodology by a group but also signals that the writer approves of this ownership.

ARGOT

An argot is a vocabulary or selection of IDIOM, which is (supposedly) not intelligible to those who are not members of the group using this language. The word is frequently, although not necessarily, associated with the underworld and hence sometimes is intended to carry the suggestion that its use is a deliberate attempt to be incomprehensible to those not members of the group. Thus for a writer to describe something as "argot" is to impute the negatives associated with secrecy, plotting, and so forth. Ironically, however, the entertainment media have made such argots part of their stock-in-trade. Rock and rap music and Mafia movies have employed the argots of organized crime, drugs, ethnic solidarity, and even surf talk to such an extent that the coded communications have become, as it were, public domain. As example, here are a few words that might at one time have been considered argot and are, at least rhetorically, used as if they still are: *wack, score, hit, line, man, gnarly, piece, packed,* and of much older distribution, *honky, gringo, suit,* and *straight.*

ARGUMENT

Argument is understood as opposed to ASSERTION and refers to a set of statements (some of which are often assumed rather than stated directly [see ENTHYMEME]) from which a conclusion is held to follow. In rhetoric the term is not restricted to the usual "argument with" or "don't argue with me" structure that assumes that an argument *for* something is necessarily an argument *against* something else. Argument at some point always *involves* assertion (each PREMISE, for instance, is an assertion) but presents these premises as evidence for the conclusion offered. Typically, arguments are classified as either INDUCTIVE or DEDUCTIVE (also see SYLLOGISM).

ASSERTION

To assert something is simply to say that it is so or is not so. If one says that something is so insistently enough, or often enough, one is sometimes believed. An assertion *is not an argument* and consequently depends for its acceptability on the credibility of the writer or on its being believed by the intended audience. Is the writer's *saying* that such and such is true sufficient to make a given reader believe it? Is what the writer is asserting commonly enough believed by the intended audience that it does not need to be argued? The premises of an argument, the statements on which the argument is based or from which the conclusion is held to follow, are assertions. So although an assertion is not an argument, arguments are composed of assertions from which a conclusion is drawn. See PREMISE and SYLLOGISM.

It may be helpful to think of asserting (making an assertion) as occupying a position on the strong end of a series of words dealing with the relative assurance or tentativeness with which a given position is presented. That tentativeness, although assertion is associated with a "strong" statement, is usually not associated with weakness but rather with the goal of solving a problem. Presenting something firmly or loudly does not make one correct and, indeed, depending on the audience, may produce doubt in cases where something stated as a suggestion or as a possibility would not. Here is one of a number of possible word lists ranging from most accommodating (least assertive) to most assertive.

offer
suggest
submit
present
propound
propose

claim
state
assert

See ROGERIAN ARGUMENT and ACCOMMODATION.

ASSOCIATION, ARGUMENT FROM

The argument from association is allied to the *AD POPULUM* ARGUMENT and sometimes to the *AD HOMINEM* CIRCUMSTAN-TIAL. To argue that X must be a criminal because she is continually seen in the company of known felons is an argument from association (we popularly know this as "guilt by association"). X could, however, be a criminologist, a sociologist, a parole officer, and so forth. To put an item in a list of things commonly held to be good is also association (we might call it "virtue by association"). Of course, the applications of this are not limited to people. To talk, for instance, about "astrology, spirit mediums, palm reading, phrenology, orgone machines, and psychoanalysis" is to "assert" an association between psychoanalysis and the other items of the list that are commonly regarded as discredited. Hence the attempt to establish this association is negatively loaded against psychoanalysis. See LOADED DICTION.

ASSUMPTION

Assumption has a number of different senses. A SURD, for instance, is an assumption—that which we accept for the moment so that the argument can proceed. Often we find the word *assumption* used in the same way as *opinion*, that is, to derogate the statement in question, as in "That's just an assumption." The problem here is that an "assumption" is in this case usually being compared to a "fact," and again usually in a naive way (see FACT). In rhetoric it is not sufficient to object to a given statement on the simple basis that it is an assumption. The question is, instead, whether the statement is an *unwarranted* assumption (see WARRANT), an *unjustified* assumption, a *naive* assumption, and so forth.

ATTRIBUTION

To attribute a statement of a position to a particular source is a frequently used rhetorical device, and as with many other devices it can be used either positively or negatively. My favorite example occurs in Orwell's "Politics and the English Language": "Our civilisation is decadent and our language—so the argument runs—must inevitably share in the general collapse. It follows that any struggle against the abuse of language is a sentimental archaism, like preferring candles to electric light or hansom cabs to aeroplanes." It is unlikely that anyone actually stated the position that Orwell attributes to "the argument" in quite this way, but Orwell uses the organic "decadence" (decay) metaphor to provide an occasion for his suggested substitution of a mechanical metaphor (language as "an instrument which we shape for our own purposes") rather than an organism that will (like all organisms) inevitably die. One might approach this as a STRAW MAN ARGUMENT, but it functions also as an example of how attribution can be used to the detriment of one's opposition. It should be noted that in the presentation of the "argument" Orwell neither identifies a particular group of people with it nor gives any particular indication of his negative view of it. Indeed, students who have read the essay carelessly will often say that Orwell believes that the language is decadent (probably because it is so commonplace to say that our civilization is decadent and that it seems obvious that our language is a part of our civilization).

Most often an essayist will use attribution to either distance herself from or reinforce a position. It is vital to the rhetorical analyst to distinguish between occasions where the writer is speaking in her own voice and those where she is attributing a statement to another. A position to be incorporated, endorsed, partially endorsed, or attacked may be presented over a fairly lengthy part of an essay, with only a brief statement before or after indicating that it does not originate from the essayist herself.

AUTHORITY, ARGUMENT FROM   (LATIN FORM, *AD VERICUNDIUM*)

The argument from authority is complex in that it raises the question of who constitutes an authority, especially if two "experts" will testify to opposite conclusions. But it is additionally complicated when the "authority" invoked is held to be supernatural or to be speaking for the supernatural. For instance, appeals for "civil disobedience" often refer to disobeying a law of distinctly human origin in favor of obeying a "higher" law. The problem comes in dealing with the *ETHOS* of the person telling us what that "higher" law is or where it is to be found and what it means. For instance, the statement "God tells us to . . . " or "The Bible tells us that . . . " raises the question "According to whom?" This can be fairly tricky. When, for instance, on the death of a pope, the college of cardinals casts ballots on who from their number will be the new pope, Roman Catholic theology does not see the process as voting, but rather as moving toward the revelation of the will of God. Thus the cardinals do not express *their* authority but instead "reveal" the authority of God. On the temporal plane the question of authority, as earlier, is complicated by there being no such thing as a "final" authority and, consequently, arguments from authority being met by arguments from other authorities. What is important to bear in mind here is that an argument from authority has never **PROVED** anything. This is hardly to say, however, that such arguments should be rejected out-of-hand; rather they should be considered in terms of the qualifications of the authority invoked to pronounce on a particular issue.

AVERAGE (NOUN)

John Paulos, in his *A Mathematician Reads the Newspaper,* tells the story of three duck hunting statisticians. The first fires six inches above the duck, and the second six inches below, at which the third exclaims, "We got it!" "In fact," we might say, they missed it. But "in fact," because ducks are hunted with shotguns, it is likely that the spread of the pellets from the combined shots was sufficient to bring down the duck (that double the "average" number of pellets in twelve-gauge bird shot spread to x diameter at a range of y meters would suffice for a bird of z size). In Garrison Keillor's Lake Woebegone, all the children are above average, and one can, with similar logic, argue that some sort of a B is the "average" grade in college courses. These things depend, of course, on how we define that apparently unambiguous term *average.* What is average depends on what you are counting, what, in other words, defines the parameters of your database. Although it is a joke, it is *possible* for all the children who inhabit a given town to be above average, provided that the population from which the average was derived was considerably larger than just the population of children in the town itself. It is frequently important to distinguish between the average (mean) and the middle (median, the point at which there are equal numbers above and below the figure given).

We seem to face in two distinct directions concerning our uses of the notion of "average." On the one hand, we deplore the average as being humdrum, everyday, without "distinction" of any sort. On the other, the "man in the street," the "average American," the "people," and the "public" are revered as a democracy's source of strength and wisdom. See STATISTICS.

Bear in mind, moreover, the conceptual difficulties involved in the concept of "average" when other than a numerical value is intended. Of what race is the average person, what gender, what political views? We could presumably come up with figures for weight, height, age, and IQ, but beyond that the concept is nearly insupportable. By one measure, for instance, given that women outnumber men, the average "person" has slightly less than one testicle. And if one is to utilize greatest number to establish the representative average (rather than a "construct"), and if one is not to be parochial, the "man in the street" is an Asian woman. See BALANCE.

BACKING
Backing is material offered in support of a particular claim. Those new to rhetorical analysis will frequently assume that an argument is weak on the basis that the writer doesn't "back up" particular statements. In so doing the analyst ignores the complexities involved with TARGET AUDIENCE. *Backing* is, for practical purposes, synonymous with *grounds,* except that in schemas for argument based on the Toulminic model, *backing* is offered in support of the WARRANT, and *grounds* directly support the claim. See EVIDENCE.

BALANCE
Newscasts and editorials often call for a more "balanced" view of whatever subject it is that they are discussing. To have, for instance, a panel of only whites discussing racism in the United States would be seen as "unbalanced" on the face of it. The analyst should be aware, however,

that whatever "balance" might be achieved, the whole notion relates, like "objectivity," to trying to achieve an *appearance* of what is conceptually unachievable. Would a "balanced" discussion of racism include an equal number of women and men of each race to be "represented"? Would the women, say, have to be equally distributed in terms of liberality or conservatism? How many anarchists should be present? How many Native American tribes should be represented? Should gay Asians be included? Many of the same problems are encountered here as are encountered with the concept of the "average" citizen. See AVERAGE, OBJECTIVE, and SUBJECTIVE.

BEGGING THE QUESTION   (ALSO CALLED CIRCULAR ARGUMENT; IN LATIN, *PETITIO PRINCIPII*)

"You have to let me into this class, I am a graduating senior" begs the question. The person making this argument is not a "graduating senior" but rather wants to be. In order to become a graduating senior, she must not only be admitted to the class but also pass it and whatever else she is taking. Ronald Reagan's reply to the questions about unconfirmed rumors concerning Dukakis's medical history ("Look, I'm not going to pick on an invalid") is a clear example of begging the question. "I must be telling the truth because I am not a liar" is circular in that it is the truth of the statement that is in question. That one has not yet been caught in a lie is no particular indication that one is not lying now. To beg the question thus is *to build the desired answer into the question itself* or, in answering a question, *to present the conclusion as a premise of the argument* for the conclusion. To "beg" the question, to follow the metaphor, is to fail to "earn" the conclusion sought. The conclusion is included within the premises that the reader is asked by the argument to grant.

The words in the left column that follow, when used to introduce a piece of information, carry with them the assumption that the information being provided is correct, true, and/or accurate. Plug them into the blank in the sentence "Smith _____ that race-based admissions programs are good for the country." Then perform the same exercise with the right column, which is composed of words that do not beg the question of the correctness, truth, and/or accuracy of the statement.

argues persuasively	argues
ascertains	asserts
demonstrates	assumes
confirms	believes
illustrates	claims
makes clear	indicates
points out	intimates
proves	says
reveals	states
shows	suggests
provides conclusive evidence	

A question like "What is the meaning of life?" provides an example of another sort of begging the question. What the rhetorical analyst needs to ask here is "What questions are begged by the question that is asked—that is, what assumptions are built into the question itself?" Like the COMPLEX QUESTION, but in a less specific sense, questions frequently beg other questions, sometimes deliberately, sometimes naively. The medieval philosopher, for example, did not ask, "Is there a God?" The question instead was "What is the nature of God?" Similarly, the question begged by "What is the meaning of life?" is that it avoids asking the necessarily prior question "Does life have meaning?" See TAUTOLOGY.

BIOLOGICAL DETERMINISM

Few people actually occupy the position that could be described as full-fledged biological determinist. Nevertheless, the position occupies a considerable amount of space in the world of argument. My father, for instance, firmly believed (he was a law enforcement officer) that there is such a thing as "the criminal element" and believed just as firmly that crime could be taken care of if criminals were put in jail (and kept there). The equation is simple. Identify members of the "criminal element," incarcerate them, and there will be no crime. He was not alone in this thinking. There is a stand-up comedy routine in which the comedian Steve Guttenberg represents himself as a southern sheriff in New York at the "Bullet Convention." He describes current law enforcement concerns such as identifying the "potential murderer" and comments something to the effect that "Hell, we don't have that problem down south. Why, just last week I was out in the woods and ran into a potential murderer. I shot the son of a bitch. He'll never kill anybody."

An essential problem with biological determinism is that, if it is true, there is nothing to be done except eliminate or incarcerate the "potential" deviants from whatever is taken to constitute the "norm" and that what constitutes that "norm" is utterly dependent upon who is doing the norming, who decides, that is, what "normal" is. The concern of the rhetorical analyst is to determine what the position forwarded assumes about the target audience's presumptions concerning biological determinism and its opposition to or combination with SOCIAL CONSTRUCTIONISM. Essential to all these sorts of thinking is the creation of a normative TROPE, of some figure or combination of figures that represents what "normal" is.

BOILERPLATE

Boilerplate refers to the content of standard disclaimers included with merchandise and "plug-in" written filler materials of any sort. To call a piece of writing "boilerplate" thus is to treat it as an arbitrary or obligatory space filler. In Seinfeldian argot, it is the "yada yada" part of any document.

BRAINWASHING

The term *brainwashing* came into common usage in English during the Korean War to "explain" why some American soldiers captured by the North Koreans made pro-Communist statements and allowed the statements to be broadcast and printed. Presumably no "real" American would do such a thing, so the Mandarin term that translates as "wash brain" was enlisted as the technique used to accomplish this unthinkable conversion.

The term thus is usually intended to mean "an insidious method of producing a particular mind-set in relation to the desired outcome of the brainwasher" (which closely resembles the naive view of what "rhetoric" is for). The methodology is fairly simple. The "washer" first attempts to dominate the information field of the "washee." In a prisoner situation the washee can be isolated from whatever is familiar to her and then bombarded with information counter to her established beliefs. This produces a high level of discomfort and anxiety in that what the washee has heretofore taken for granted is now subject to doubt, even rendered unacceptable, or no longer credible (think back, for instance, to a time when you remember having found that something you had taken for granted was not true). In the SOCRATIC METHOD this corresponds to the *elenchus,* the "refutation."

It would seem that the human mind has difficulty maintaining itself without some sort of schema or organizational grid with which to organize those data available to it that it will understand as "reality." At the point where one reality system has been rendered untenable, the mind apparently is unjudgmentally susceptible to whatever system presents itself in order to find relief from this discomfort. (This is the opposite impulse to what the poet John Keats described as "negative capability," the ability to remain in a condition of uncertainty without seeking to reconcile conflicting views with an overarching theory.)

BUZZ WORD

Buzz word derives from drug argot referring to a pleasant feeling, as in "a nice buzz." Buzz words are found more frequently in speech than in writing because their repetition is more obvious in writing. Buzz words are used to impress the reader or auditor with the importance and the expertise of the user. They tend to go in and out of fashion fairly quickly once their "buzz" quality is consciously noticed. One such dying buzz word is *excited*. Administrese (the special language spoken by administrators to nonadministrators) used to be full of "We are very *excited* about...." Some seem to be noticing that better work could probably be done in a calmer state. A former university-system chancellor provides an example of the use of the administrative buzz word in this quotation from the *Houston Insider:*

> Our view is that the delegation was wonderfully *focused* behind us on these problems as they began to unfold in the legislative session. One of the things we learned was that in a time of stable or declining support for education, it's not just the legislative process that must be *focused* upon but indeed the whole formula process, because 75 to 80 percent

> of education funding comes through formula funding. We have not traditionally been as *focused* on what happens in the formula committees of the coordinating board as we need to be and have begun to be. [my italics]

Additionally buzz words are those used to name the latest area of concern, especially within particular professional or political groups, so the "buzz" is what is going around at the moment. The term *politically correct* is an interesting example. It was originally used as a term of insult to a set of supposedly liberal ideas about fostering social equality through avoidance of negative designations (*remedial,* for instance, became *developmental,* etc.). I now see the term used regularly and without any hint of irony as meaning "appropriately sensitive." *Innovation* was big a year or so ago; *diversity* looks as if it will be with us for a good while, along with *collaborative learning projects.* See HOT-BUTTONS.

CACOGRAPHY
The rhetorical effect that the writer of cacography usually seeks is to denigrate, by association with the subliterate, the subject so represented. For instance: "Iff yu dont join the Nashunul Rifle Asoshiashun we will kill yu." Rhetorically considered, cacography is deliberately bad spelling.

CHARACTERIZATION, EVALUATIVE
Arguably I should not use the word *evaluative* here in that characterization is *inherently* evaluative. I chose to do so for the reader looking over the scan list in order to find a name for this subcategory of NAMING. To "characterize" a person or an organization, typically one names a "characteristic" behavior. The following series is intended to illustrate how highly charged words indicate varying evaluative stances toward what may be *the same behavior.*

I will begin with the example presented in the entry for
LOADED DICTION.

firm	stubborn	obstinate	obstructionist
confident	self-centered	closed-minded	egotistical
dedicated	committed	militant	possessed
cooperative	dependent	parasitic	sycophantic
self-sufficient	independent	idiosyncratic	antisocial
aggressive	quarrelsome	combative	sadistic
expressive	dramatic	melodramatic	hysterical
unpretentious	unsophisticated	ill-mannered	rude
generous	selfless	self-sacrificing	passive-aggressive
observant	watchful	suspicious	paranoid

CIRCULAR ARGUMENT

The columnist Charles Krauthammer argues that one
should wish one's children to grow up to be heterosexual
because life is hard enough, but "Gay life is particularly
hard." The argument resembles that of the person who is
glad that she does not like caviar, because if she did like it
she would eat a lot of it, and she hates the stuff. That is,
Krauthammer appears to be oblivious to the "hardness" of
gay life being directly related to the intolerance of heterosexuals, which he is supporting the continuance of.
If, in other words, gay life were *not* particularly hard,
Krauthammer would not be able to argue against it. See
BEGGING THE QUESTION and TAUTOLOGY.

CIRCUMLOCUTION

A circumlocution is a talking "around" a subject rather
than addressing it directly. Like a EUPHEMISM, a circumlocution is difficult to identify precisely because to so label
a verbal construction presumes evasion as the intent of the
writer. To say, "The candidate's diction was not as consid-
erate of the gender mix of the group as it might have been
had he been more sensitive to its essentially conservative

posture" would be a circumlocution for "The candidate talked dirty." A circumlocution can, of course, be an attempt to avoid giving offense. See TACT.

CLAIM

In discussions of argument the word *claim* has at least two distinct meanings. If one is discussing argument from the perspective of Stephen Toulmin's work (see WARRANT), the word *claim* refers to what most people would call the THESIS of the argument. For the extra-Toulminic discussion, however, a claim is a taking possession of something or declaration of position and may thus be used as support for the thesis instead of constituting the thesis. See also QUALIFICATION.

CLICHÉ   (CLI *SHAY*)

A cliché is a FIGURE OF SPEECH that has been used so often that sophisticated readers regard its use as tantamount to an admission of mindlessness. Recognizing your own use of them is often difficult (avoiding clichés is "more easily said than done") because they are so often used as to have become almost automatic ("second nature"). Any list of clichés must become quickly superseded ("out of date"); it must constantly be added to ("updated") so that "as far as clichés go" we are unlikely to ever get to "the bottom line," especially considering "today's fast-paced lifestyles." "But there is no rest for the weary in sight at this point in time."

The point here is that we should "avoid clichés like the plague" and most particularly those we are tempted to put in quotation marks (unless, of course, we are trying to illustrate the fatuousness of the cliché). Writers, however, will often use clichés as a point of discussion or entry into an argument. Evaluation of such use is typically dependent upon the reader's estimation of the writer's consciousness of using a cliché. Some very naive arguments use clichés in the same way other naive arguments use the term COMMON SENSE—that is, as accepted wisdom. Most often, however, to label something a cliché is to attempt to discredit it. One implies that the expression so labeled is so commonplace that its users or consumers have suspended any critical response to it, that their response is, in other words, "knee-jerk" as opposed to considered.

Having said this, however, the analyst must always consider who the target audience is and consider as well that clichés are clichés because they are used frequently, which indicates that many people are comfortable with them. The writer can then work easily within this comfort zone, if we may so call it, most frequently to argue in favor of traditional (and poorly defined) concepts such as, say, "common decency," "family values," "simple civility," "good manners," and so forth. Given that a central tenet of rhetorical analysis is that the writer is always given the benefit of the doubt, we must assume that the user of the cliché *knows* that it is a cliché and that, if we react badly to it, we more than likely have an indication that we are not members of the target audience. Consider further that in some English as a Second Language classes students are deliberately taught clichés because they are so commonplace, such a part of the everyday currency of communication.

COLLOQUIAL

Colloquial language is that language characteristic of speaking as opposed to writing, and particularly the sort of speaking that would be involved in a conversation. Thus it is informal and often contains the hesitations and restatements that are characteristic of a conversation. Gilbert Highet is affecting the colloquial when he writes in his essay "The *Gettysburg Address*": "There are many descriptions of Lincoln, all showing the same curious blend of grandeur and awkwardness, or lack of dignity, or–it would be best to call it humility." Highet, presumably, wishes to create the effect of immediacy, as if he is groping, in the immediate presence of the reader and the multiple accounts of the day, for the right word. Contractions (*can't, won't*, etc.) are also characteristic of the colloquial. The writer wishes to convey a sense of directness and simplicity–the opposite of what "fancy" writing might be. Use of the colloquial often constitutes a part of an *AD POPULUM* ARGUMENT, as in, for instance, "I'm just a simple man, Your Honor, and I don't have any fancy education, but my momma taught to me to recognize a liar when I hear one." Also see VERNACULAR and *ETHOS*.

COMMON SENSE
This is a variation on the *ad populum* argument. "Common sense" tells us that the sun "rises" in the east and "sets" in the west. Current astronomy indicates that the sun doesn't "rise" at all. Any appeal to "common sense" should be treated with great suspicion because it is usually a cover for a weak argument. "Common sense" told us that "what goes up must come down," but we know that if we throw it high enough, it won't. To endorse something by saying that it is "only common sense" constitutes an example of positively LOADED DICTION. See SAYING.

COMPLEX QUESTION
"Do you still frown at small children?" and "Do you still cheat at cards?" and the classic "Do you still beat your wife?" are intended to invoke a *single* (yes or no) answer when to answer the question with only a single answer would confirm a built-in assertion. The complex question

is essentially a trick and, if recognized as such, is properly answered by dividing it into its elements and replying to each of them, that is, "I do not now nor have I ever cheated at cards." The complex question is also sometimes called a "loaded" question. The parliamentary motion to divide the question (and to thus discuss and vote on it a part at a time) is a recognition of the need to separate issues and assumptions. See BEGGING THE QUESTION.

COMPLEX STATEMENT

This is very closely related to the complex question, and, again, it is essentially a trick. Ronald Reagan's "There you go again" in his televised debate with Jimmy Carter when Carter had given a complex answer to a seemingly simple question is an example. The complex statement assumes that there is a present error that is indisputable and that it is only one of a whole series of such, the contents of which series is unspecified. "TV journalism appears to be up to its old tricks" is a simpler example. We are back again to begging the question. To respond to the statement "TV journalism appears to be up to its old tricks" requires that one first deal with the asserted (not argued) guilt of TV in the past and then to assert that it *isn't* now doing what it *didn't* do in the past. Despite the doubled negatives, it should be clear that to defend against a charge that was implied but never stated puts one at a considerable psychological disadvantage.

COMPLICATE

A so-called "simplification" can be referred to as "simplistic" or "over-simple" when it is seen as obscuring or distorting the original rather than clarifying it. The drive of argument is quite frequently toward that "simplification." The drive to simplify is exemplified in the SOUND BITE and its journalistic equivalents. Consequently the rhetor who suggests that she needs to "complicate" the issue will usually apologize for the "necessity" of doing so.

Part of the problem may be evident from the complexity of the language's relation to the word *simple*. We use it in combination with *pure* for emphasis, as in "pure and simple," and we use it to denote feeblemindedness, as in *simpleton* and *simpleminded*. From the perspective of rhetoric, writing is never pure and rarely, if ever, simple. When the rhetor presents "objectivity" and "straightforwardness" as rhetorical poses, for instance, she "complicates" matters that the rhetorically less informed would like to think of, if at all, as "simple." To "complicate," as a mode of argument, then, is to present the argument under attack as misleading precisely because it is "simple."

CONCESSION

As we use the word in "to concede the point," a *concession* is an acceptance, or the appearance of acceptance, of at least part of an opposing position. Although it is not always the case, a concession is often made as if something were being given up for the sake of harmony (although indeed the point may have been accepted from the outset). This relies on the ancient notion that "turnabout is fair play," that is, I gave up something to you, now you should give up something to me. When this strategy is operative, it is often signaled by the request for fairness being put in the form of a polite question. "I can agree that the educational system is a large contributor to the state of current morality, but might not other factors be considered as well?" (the writer can then go on and present factors that may very well render "the educational system" a minor player). Although it doesn't happen as often in writing as in speech, sometimes a seemingly total concession will be made, and then the writer will go on to reinterpret what she has agreed to (having, she hopes, temporarily gotten the opposition to lower its guard in the face of her agreement). In speech the tactic runs something like "I agree with everything you have said, *and* . . ." (at which point the speaker goes on to draw a very different conclusion from that of the party with whom she agreed). Typically this is done for the benefit of those who have not taken a position in the hope that the agreed-with party will not know how to reply (for the reason that the argument she gave earlier was *agreed* upon, at least apparently).

CONCRETE

See ABSTRACT. The "concrete," for Orwell, is the word or phrase that calls up a particularized visual image. "Shot in the back of the neck" is Orwell's famous example. The chosen words attempt to limit reader response to the specific. There are, however, degrees of concreteness. The word *courage* is abstract, *courage under fire* is less abstract, but neither has a specific corporeal correspondent. *Mother* can be argued to have a corporeal correspondent, but on analysis even it does not and is less concrete than *gray-haired mother. Your mother* and *my mother,* on the other hand, do have corporeal correspondents and are correspondingly concrete. Arguably, the more concrete an example is, the less possibility exists for misunderstanding. It may also be argued, however, that the more concrete an example is, the less it lends itself to generalization. See LADDER OF ABSTRACTION.

CONNOTATION

Connotation is typically opposed to *denotation,* and the opposition stresses emotional responses to a word versus the so-called DICTIONARY meaning. In contemporary rhetoric the opposition is naive on several grounds. In the first place, there is no such thing as "the dictionary"; rather there are a *number* of dictionaries, no one of which can claim to be authoritative (which is one of the reasons that this is a glossary and not a dictionary). Hence the "denotative" meaning of a word can, at best, be only approximated (lacking the "big book in the sky" of which all dictionaries in this world would be imperfect imitations). Hence one cannot, except in a very imprecise manner, talk about what a given word "really" means. This is further complicated by words changing meaning over time–the principle that the *Oxford English Dictionary* (*OED*) is based on. Etymological dictionaries, which theorize about "origins" of words, do not give us what words "really" mean either, but rather collect current theory on where a given word originated and what its "original" meaning might have been. What we may understand from the word *connotation* is no less complex. Most often definitions will refer to what a word "suggests" as opposed to what it "explicitly" says. If we take this to mean that a given word, then, has a "connotative meaning," we are even worse off than we were with "denotation." Consider, for instance, what the "connotative" meaning of the word *bottle* might be–what it might "suggest" to the teetotaling spouse of an alcoholic and what it might "suggest" to the parent of a six-month-old child. Finally, *every* individual at *any* given time exists in a similar "special" relationship to given words. Hence any notion of there being one specific connotative meaning for a particular word is insupportable. Be sure, then, in any discussion involving these terms to constantly bear in mind that *both* words of necessity refer to multiple, rather than single, meanings. See LOADED DICTION and CHARACTERIZATION.

CONSENSUS

Consensus comes to us as a rhetorical term largely from the perspectives offered to rhetorical theory by feminism. The essential claim is that women's rhetorical goals are different from men's in that women most frequently aim for community, whereas men aim for domination (winning). As rhetorical analysts we need to consider that consensus is a goal that a particular argument can set for itself regardless of the gender of the writer, and moreover that consensus, given the audience targeted, may distinctly not be the rhetorical goal of particular arguments. See especially ROGERIAN ARGUMENT.

CONSISTENCY

Ralph Waldo Emerson once famously wrote, "A foolish consistency is the hobgoblin of little minds. . . ." And nearly as famously Walt Whitman responded, "Do I contradict myself? / Very well then I contradict myself, / (I am large, I contain multitudes . . .)." Nevertheless, under the sway of the argument from REASON, we hold consistency to be basic to sound argument. However, ROGERIAN ARGUMENT, in that it can incorporate a number of frames of reference and treat them, or at least appear to treat them, with equal respect, comes close to the Whitmanic pronouncement in that it appears to value a multiplicity of opinion and accepts solutions only contingently, for the time being, rather than as absolute answers.

The rhetorical analyst should be alert to the use of the claim of inconsistency as a major tactic of the counterargument. *A*, for instance, will claim that *B* is inconsistent in, say, supporting a politician accused of sexual indiscretions and claiming to be a feminist. Frequently such an argument is to the point that *both* positions (feminism and the position favoring the politician) are thereby weakened, or even shown to be untenable. But, as with the demonstration that a syllogism is invalid (see VALID), nothing whatever has been established about the worth of either position. Rather, a claim has been made that one cannot hold both positions simultaneously, which says nothing at all about whether either or both of them are true or false. See HYPOCRISY, ACCUSATION OF.

DEADPAN
As a mode of delivery, deadpan is familiar to us as the manner of the comedian who delivers material without changing expression, straight-faced. The writing mode from which this is probably borrowed (in one of the few cases where a mode of speaking borrows from a mode of writing) is the methodology of the satirist (see SATIRE). Considering satire as a complex and extended exercise in irony, the deadpan delivery allows a writer to develop a theme at considerable length without "losing" the audience. When the approach works, the audience becomes complicit in the irony in that it continues to pay attention to the writer in the hope that she will lose control of the straight face, in the same way that the comedian can break down and begin to laugh (apparently) in spite of herself. Vital to the approach, however, is that the reader recognize that the writer is employing a PERSONA, an assumed character, rather than speaking in her own voice.

DEBATE
Although one often hears debate referred to in the terms used to discuss argument, debate is no more argument than Olympic fencing is sword-fighting. In the loose use of the term, *debate* refers to an arena of discussion ("the current debate concerning vouchers in primary education"), and often inherent in the reference is an attempt to

valorize the subject as fit for discussion. Take, for instance, the phrase "in the recent debate concerning 'smokers' rights.'" There are, of course, no such things as "smokers' rights," but to involve the concept within the respectability of "debate" (usually understood as a "fair" contest between competing positions) it is intended to create existential import for one of the (always two) positions. See EITHER/OR and EXISTENTIAL IMPORT. Understood formally, debates are forensic contests between two individuals, or teams, under a particular set of rules and subject to some sort of judging or scoring. Unlike the logic it may involve, argument has no rules, nor can it in any real way be "scored," despite the idea of "market surveys."

DEDUCTIVE ARGUMENT

A deductive argument in a CATEGORICAL SYLLOGISM moves from the general to the particular. The classic example is "All men are mortal; Socrates is a man; therefore Socrates is mortal." The argument makes an assertion applicable to *every* member of a SET, asserts that the being in question is a member of the set, and then concludes that that being is governed by the original assertion. Deductive argument, given that we are willing to accept the truth of the premises and that the argument is valid, is held to yield truth. If, for instance, Socrates lived forever, the error would lie in the assertion that Socrates is a man. If he lives forever we know that he cannot be a man simply because all men die (are mortal). We should here note, however (see PROOF), that we are not the only people who will never know if Socrates could live forever. There is *no time* at which we (or our descendants) can say that the conditions of the statement have been met (i.e., the only way the conditions could be met would be for "forever" to be in the past).

DEFINITION

The statement "America: love it or leave it" involves large questions of definition. How is one supposed to define "America" or "love"? A reply to this sort of thing might be to say, "I express my love of my country by seeking to right those things that are wrong with it. I choose not to accept the definition of 'love' that suggests that I must unconditionally accept any action of a given president or that these actions can be automatically defined as a part of 'America.'" Many arguments dissolve when the participants are simply asked to define their terms. It has been argued that the question of definition is so important that finally *all* argument depends on it. That depends, of course, on your definition of "definition." In any case definition, or an aspect of it, is likely to be close to the core of most arguments you will encounter. Consider the importance of how one defines terms like *crime, poverty,* or even *race* (which conception gave Hitler a lot of problems–he is reputed to have referred at one time to the Japanese as "our Aryan brothers"). The obviousness of the problem with this latter is putting the U.S. census takers in a position similar to those who devised the rules for apartheid in South Africa. If my mother were Amerindian and (native) African, and my father were born in Puerto Rico of an Italian father and a mother who, although a British citizen, was of Chinese ancestry, how am I to fill out my census question? This example is extreme, but no one can sensibly claim the "purity" that the census seems to ask for. Or, if it doesn't ask for purity, it seems to ask for the "dominant" race in one's genealogy (which is "defined" as the opposite of the most "powerful"–that is, when we are told that the mortality rate for "black" infants is double that of "white" infants, we are to understand by "black" any of an infinite variety of racial combinations, but by "white" only those *apparently* outside that "mix").

DEFINITIVE
The "definitive" is "the last word on the subject" or "complete" and even "authoritative" (see AUTHORITY). The emphasis on finality implicit in the word (it does not make much sense, for instance, to say, "This is, at the moment, definitive") has been largely replaced by the attitude expressed by the phrase "state of the art," and its implicit "at this time."

DEMONIZE
To demonize is to invoke an either/or argument in which all or the greatest part of the ills of the world are blamed on a specific source or a set of sources identifiable as adherent to a given set of conscienceless evils. (Perhaps the most famous instance of this is Ronald Reagan's characterization of the Soviet Union as the "evil empire.") *They* are the forces of darkness. *We* are the forces of light. To demonize is to attempt to cast the opponents of some position in an argument in this way. Demonizing is a common tactic of the STRAW MAN ARGUMENT in that typically another is made the object of attack in order to distract from a weakness in the argument being presented. It is one of the most obvious of the APPEALS TO FEAR.

DEMOTIC
This term shares the Greek root with *democracy,* meaning government of "the people." It carries two meanings, "simple" and "ordinary," either or both of which can be intended by the writer using the word. "The demotic," or demotic language, would be that which would be

understandable to "ordinary" people. As such it would differ from EDUCATED USAGE.

DEVIL'S ADVOCATE, PLAY THE

In order to play the devil's advocate, one must declare that one is so doing. The writer claims thus that the position she is presenting is not hers (indeed, the position represents the most threatening of the opposing positions) but a position that needs to be taken into consideration in the process of formulating the best possible defense of the position "really" being advocated. Because the writer is representing herself as on the same side as the reader (and thus only "playing" devil's advocate), she can potentially gain the freedom not only to present in detail but also to explore ideas that would otherwise be rejected outright. I might not listen to X, but I might well listen to someone explain how X thinks.

Although it need not be so used, it places the writer in a position from which she can create a great deal of sympathy for and promote familiarity with a position that, were it not being so presented, would be rejected out of hand. Typically, the more familiar we are with a position, the more comfortable we can be with it, the more tolerant of it we can be. Thus the writer who claims to be playing the devil's advocate may have a hidden agenda. She may in fact *be* the devil's advocate.

DIALECT

A dialect is a manner of pronunciation and often grammatical arrangement that is characteristic of a region or a racial or ethnic group. Dialect is employed intentionally when the speaker or writer wishes to invoke whatever ambiance or *ETHOS* she believes the target audience will associate with the region or group invoked. The aim may also be to establish an identification between the target audience and the writer (i.e., the writer would like the audience members to believe that she is one of them). Most often a writer will move into dialect rather than STANDARD ENGLISH as a means of ridiculing the position presented. In American English, however, the matter is complicated by the tradition of the wise bumpkin, the "country boy" who is sharper than the city slicker. See COLLOQUIAL, EYE DIALECT, and VERNACULAR.

DIALOGUE

A dialogue is a verbal interchange between two or more people. It typically implies civil conversation on a given subject designed to promote understanding and as such is sometimes used as a verb ("we need to dialogue about that"). A dialogue can also be a representation of such an exchange (as in a play, or in the "Platonic Dialogues"). In this latter form it is set up from the outset to promote a particular position. Thus the rhetorical purpose of dialogue in writing is to give the appearance that more than one position is being represented in an effort to come to the best possible conclusion. See MONOLOGUE.

DICTION

Diction means simply "word choice." Hence it is fruitless to say that a writer uses diction in her argument. This is the same as saying that she uses words, or worse, that she uses logic. The question always comes down to "What *kind* of diction?" *Some* of the terms that can be used to describe an author's diction are *slang, colloquial, informal, formal, heightened, poetic, pretentious, fey, Latinate, Anglo Saxon.* The list goes on and on. Like TONE, diction can be almost endlessly described.

DICTION, LEVELS OF

The idea that there are levels of diction presumes that one would speak in a different way to a five-year-old than one would to a university president, or that one would speak differently to one's peers in an informal setting (say, a bar) than one would to a judge in a formal setting (say, her court). We presume thus that certain "levels" of diction are more appropriate than others in a given social situation. The difference between the retort "Bullshit" and the retort "I disagree" involves levels of diction. Very often writers will use several levels of diction within a given essay, and the analyst must consequently be careful about pronouncing too quickly on the level used. Given levels can be variously named, but traditional classifications include formal, colloquial, heightened (for ceremonial occasions), informal, and so forth. Less traditional, but still useful, are, among many others, locker room, baby talk, street, classroom, and lecture hall.

DICTIONARY, THE

It is a commonplace that *the* meanings of words can be found in *the* dictionary. There is, in *this* world anyway, no such thing. As I write this I have within a few feet of me the *Oxford English Dictionary,* New Edition; *Webster's Seventh New Collegiate Dictionary;* the *American Heritage Electronic Dictionary of the English Language,* Third Edition; and *Webster's New International Dictionary,* Second Edition. No two of these dictionaries contain the same information, even though two of them are issued by the same publisher. As an example, take *eggshell,* as the word might be used to describe a surface: *American Heritage*–"A pale yellow to yellowish white"; *Webster's Seventh*–"slightly glossy" (with no mention of color); *Webster's New International*–"Designating a slightly glossy appearance like that of an eggshell" and as a color, "eggshell blue = robin's egg blue," "eggshell green = robin's egg blue" (which is defined under its own entry as "A color, bluish-green in hue of low saturation and high brilliance"—with no other entry for *eggshell* as color); *Oxford English Dictionary*—"a term of colour or of a paint finish intermediate between flat and glossy" (with no definition given of a particular color).

We might conclude that as a texture *eggshell* refers to a surface that is less than glossy, but what color is it? (Or, "What colour is it?" if we were British.) The answer would have to be: it depends on which dictionary you look it up in or, better, what color the person using the word means to indicate by the word.

Let us try, then, a word that refers *only* to color—*ecru*: *OED*—"the colour of unbleached linen"; *American Heritage*—"a grayish to pale yellow or light grayish-yellowish brown"; *Webster's Seventh*—"beige" (the entry for *beige* reads "a variable color averaging light grayish or yellowish brown"); *Webster's New International*—"Having the beige color of raw or unbleached stuff, as silk, linen, or the like."

The point of these examples, beyond my hope to illustrate that there is no such thing as *the* dictionary, is that dictionaries do not agree among themselves (and indeed, for reasons of copyright they *cannot* agree among themselves or else the issuer of the later dictionary would be liable to suit for plagiarism from the maker of the earlier) and further that there is no dictionary in which one can find *the* answer to the question "What does *ecru* (or, for that matter, *eggshell*) *really* mean?" Because there is no UR dictionary (the perfect and timeless dictionary of which all temporal dictionaries are imperfect copies), the only thing we can say that a word "really" means is what we intend for it to mean, which, because we have only other words to explain it, will remain forever uncertain.

DILEMMA

A dilemma is a problem that appears to have two unacceptable solutions. If I let go, you drown. If I don't let go, we both drown. The two conditions are the "horns" of the dilemma, upon which one is said to be "caught." If I vote for David Duke, I support a Nazi. If I vote for his opponent, I vote for a thief. To "go between the horns" I would move out of the state or sponsor a write-in candidate. See EITHER/OR.

DIRECT ADDRESS

One form of direct address is the OPEN LETTER in which a specific person is directly addressed in the (reading) presence of others. A more common form is that in which the reader, whoever she might be, is addressed as "you." The hoped-for effect is a sense of immediacy from the implicit request that the reader consider what is being presented personally rather than abstractly. The poet Walt Whitman gives us an example in his "Song of Myself," which is so outrageous, so transparent an indulgence in the fiction of direct address (as it must be a fiction in that the writer has no idea who the person addressed as "you" is) that it can be seen as charming and witty. He writes, beginning in line 1301 of that poem, "Listener up there! What have you to confide to me? / . . . / (Talk honestly, no one else hears you, and I stay only a minute longer.)." The reader is "up there" because that is how we read books, from above them, looking down. The humor lies in Whitman acting as if he, as a person speaking, is physically inside of the text and could hear the reader if she spoke and further, as if this is a "private" communication—that this is a relationship with a particular reader, not any reader of all those who have read the poem.

DISCOURSE, DISCOURSE COMMUNITY

Discourse, as a rhetorician would use the term, refers to the set of conventions and practices embodied in a given text or set of texts characteristic of a definable group (politicians, philosophers, critics, theologians, physicists, etc.) that "discourses" on, or discusses, particular subjects. Any one of these groups constitutes what is called a "discourse community," above which we could understand the language common to all the discourses as a "metadiscourse." The individual units, or communities, are best understood as DOMAINS. The "discourse," then, is the "discussion."

What, as rhetoricians, we call "rhetorical analysis" a linguist would call "discourse analysis." *Discourse,* however, carries with it the suggestion of a conversation, which includes argument, response, and counterresponse. Rhetoric, although it may include those, may be only the argument. To refer to a single item, then, as an example of "discourse" is to imply that it is a part of a larger structure, or set of such arguments. It may be helpful to think of *discourse* in terms of the related word *cursive,* which describes "longhand" as opposed to printed writing. The longhand ties the letters together into the units of words. Printing, in contrast, adds spacing to delineate groups of spaced letters as words. *Discourse,* like *cursive,* derives its meaning from the connections.

DISCOURSE REGISTER

Almost certainly drawn from the application of the word *register* in music, where it refers to the "range" of a particular instrument or a voice classification (tenor, soprano, baritone, etc.), the "discourse register" is that part of the total "range" of a language that is seen as appropriate to a particular social and professional linguistic practice. For the impresario to walk on stage at a symphony and ask the audience to "shut the hell up" would be to speak in an "inappropriate" discourse register.

DISJUNCTIVE SYLLOGISM

One of the three types of formal syllogisms (CATEGORICAL, HYPOTHETICAL, and DISJUNCTIVE; see also SYLLOGISM and PREMISE), the disjunctive takes the form "Either the paper is on my desk or in the trash can. It is not in the trash can. Therefore it is on my desk." Do not confuse the disjunctive syllogism with the problems of EITHER/OR in that the *rules* governing the disjunctive syllogism preclude the problem basic to the either/or. In the disjunctive syllogism one may arrive at a VALID conclusion only if one *denies* one of the terms. The categorical and hypothetical syllogistic forms are important to rhetoric. I mention the disjunctive only because it is the third of the three traditional forms. It is not useful in ordinary language argument.

DISTRIBUTION

A term is referred to as "distributed" in the CATEGORICAL SYLLOGISM when it is qualified by the so-called "universals" (see PREMISE), which are "All" and "No"—called "affirmative" and "negative," respectively. Thus in the statements "All cats are carnivores" and "No cats are vegetarians" the *subject* term, "cats," is "distributed." However, the *predicate* term in the universal affirmative statement ("carnivores") is *not* distributed (or, to put it more simply, it does not explicitly apply to *all* or *no* carnivores). Thus if I am told that "All cats are carnivores" and "Mack is a carnivore," I may not legitimately conclude from those statements that Mack is *therefore* a cat. The argument cannot be VALID unless the middle (repeated) term, "carnivore," is "distributed" in at least one of the PREMISES (statements on which the argument is based). Mack may, for instance, happen to be a dog, or a person. This is called the fallacy of the undistributed middle. *However,* in a *universal negative* statement, *both terms are distributed.* Consider, then, "No cats are vegetarians. Mack is a vegetarian. Therefore Mack is not a cat." The middle term, "vegetarian," is distributed in the first premise and not distributed in the second. The rule that the middle term must be distributed in *at least one premise* is satisfied. Thus we are allowed to say that the syllogism (given, of course, that all other rules of logic have been followed) is valid. In a variation of the earlier example, however, note that the conclusion does not follow: "All cats are carnivores. Fluffy is a carnivore. Therefore Fluffy is a cat." The middle term, "carnivore," is not distributed in either premise. The syllogism is therefore *invalid.* (The particular Fluffy referred to *may* in fact *be* a cat, but that cannot be concluded from *this argument*–see VALID.)

So much for distribution of the middle term. The further rule concerning distribution is that no term that is *not* distributed in the premises may be distributed in the conclusion. Consider: "All cats are carnivores; Rex is not a cat; therefore Rex is not a carnivore." The first premise is a universal affirmative. Therefore the term "cats" is distributed, but the term "carnivores" is not. The second premise is a universal negative (no Rex [members of the set "Rex"] is a cat). Therefore both the term "Rex" and the term "cat" are distributed. The conclusion is also a universal negative (no Rex [members of the set "Rex"] is a carnivore). Therefore both of its terms ("Rex" and "carnivores") are distributed. However, the term "carnivore" is *not* distributed in either premise, so we cannot distribute it in the conclusion. We can draw from the premises that information that is implicit in them but no more than that information. For a further instance, take: "Sam will unquestioningly accept anybody whom Bill likes, and Bill can't stand Roy; so don't try to tell me that Sam likes Roy." This is invalid. That Sam likes everybody Bill does *does not imply* that Sam likes *only* those people Bill likes. In a syllogism we see: "All friends of Bill are friends of Sam; no Roy (members of the set 'Roy') is a friend of Bill; therefore no Roy (members of the set 'Roy') is a friend of Sam." The syllogism is invalid because the term "friends of Sam" is distributed in the conclusion (both terms of a universal negative are distributed) but not in the premises (only the first term of a universal affirmative is distributed).

DIVISION OF THE QUESTION

In parliamentary procedure the motion to divide the question is often invoked and for numerous and complex reasons. As I write, Clinton detractors are trying to establish that *the* question is: can Bill Clinton be trusted? Their answer is no. He misled the country concerning his relationship with Monica Lewinsky and therefore cannot be trusted. Democrats answer that sexual conduct that is legal differs from political conduct and leadership capacity. They argue that many admittedly great leaders have been "morally" compromised in terms of marital fidelity and that to say that Clinton misled the public concerning sexual conduct is *a different question than his fitness to govern.* The question of Clinton's moral leadership capabilities is, and ought to be, separable from the question of his capacity as a political leader. The "misled" public, according to numerous polls, sees the matter similarly. Clinton detractors are trying to change that perception by insisting that what the public seems to see as two questions should be seen as one.

Because such matters are never clear-cut, the suggestion that a question be divided frequently gives the appearance of being cautious and sensible. After all, it could be offered, if the disputants wish to reunite the parts of the question *after* they are considered separately, they can always do so. However, if those who support the division are correct in their assumption that one of the divisions is passable and the other questionable, it is nearly impossible to make one question of them again. If one part is voted up and the other down, to reunite them is to lose both.

As in the issue of BEGGING THE QUESTION, what *the* question is is either problematic or, if it is not, can *be made* problematic.

DOMAIN

A domain is a territory or field in which a particular set of rules is held to apply. Consider, for instance, how the set "human beings" might be considered within the domains of biology, of chemistry, and of Roman Catholic theology. The idea of "domains" can be extremely useful to the rhetorical analyst in that one often finds that arguments appropriate to one domain are being applied in another where they are not appropriate. What is at issue is usually an assertion of a hierarchy of domains that, among the domains themselves (because they observe different rules), is unresolvable unless one has the political power to silence the other (i.e., to imprison or execute "blasphemers"). See DISCOURSE COMMUNITY. See also *AD BACULUM* and EXISTENTIAL IMPORT, particularly for the discussion of the term *creation science*. See especially RELATIVE.

DOUBLE ENTENDRE   (DUBBEL AHN *TAHND*)

A word or phrase that can be understood in two ways, one of which is usually sexually suggestive, is a double entendre. Rhetorically a double entendre can be used to ridicule or discredit a position that asks to be taken with high seriousness. As an aspect of tone, it can also be used for any of the reasons a joke would be thought to be appropriate.

EDUCATED USAGE

Educated usage refers to the grammar, diction, and sometimes sentence structure that would be employed by a person with particular training in an area or a general education beyond the average. In English this corresponds to what *uneducated* usage often calls "proper" English, by which is meant "correct" English. Educated usage, recognizing that "correctness" is a social construct, would use the word, as I use it here, in quotes. See STANDARD ENGLISH.

EFFECTIVE

The claim that such and such a construction or device is "effective" is so problematic that a sophisticated rhetorical analyst avoids the question altogether. In the first place the rhetorician, as opposed to the sophist (see SOPHISTRY), is not primarily interested in the effectiveness of an argument; instead she is interested in how it is intended to work and, if she is personally interested in the topic, its "soundness" (see INTENTION). Short of a very complex market analysis (and only questionably then), the extent of a given device's "effectiveness" is unavailable. Further, the "effectiveness" of any given argument is so intimately tied to the composition of its audience as to be beyond the parameters of rhetorical analysis. Insofar as rhetorical analysis is evaluative, it confines its evaluation to questions of the writer's intention (always, of course, hypothetical) and the "soundness" of the arguments presented. Thus although one can say that a particular writer is trying to influence her audience through use of an *AD POPULUM* argument (for instance), one cannot say that the use is "effective." The "effectiveness" of this or any other form of argument will depend on the mood and rhetorical sophistication of the audience, neither of which is available to the rhetorical analyst and is only problematically available to the writer.

EITHER/OR   (ALSO CALLED THE BLACK OR WHITE FALLACY OR THE BLACK AND WHITE FALLACY OR FALSE DILEMMA)
This is one of the most widespread, invidious, and deceptive of Western habits of thought. At its most obvious, it states or implies that a given item is either a member of one set or a member of that set's opposite. We aren't usually disturbed by questions that ask if we are for or against something, but this is an example of either/or. Indeed, any question or statement that divides existence or thought into two opposing camps is an example of it. The questions involved are highly complex and probably result from thinking that classified the world as "us" and "other"–on the understanding that whatever was "other" was a danger to "us." This is fostered by Aristotelian logic that suggests that there is *A* and another category, Not *A*, the two of which comprise all. Hence we get classifications like Christian and Infidel (which, because *infidel* means "unfaithful," divides the world into Christians and all others), Jew and Gentile (which, again, because *Gentile* means "non-Jew," divides the world into Jews and all others), True or False, For or Against (see DEMONIZE).

Where we are most concerned with the problem in rhetoric is in the analysis of arguments that suggest, say, that we are either against abortion or in favor of legalized murder (which last is a contradiction in terms–the term *murder* is a *legal* term for a criminal [i.e., "illegal"] act–hence "legalized" murder is no longer murder). To unload the terms, we would say, then, that we are either for abortion or against it—but the problem remains. What if we are in favor of abortion in cases of pregnancy resulting from rape or incest? What if we do not define *as* abortion any action taken before "viability" (the theoretical ability of the fetus [see DEFINITION] to survive outside the womb)? The habit carries further, however. We tend to think that if a proposition cannot be demonstrated to be true, then it is therefore untrue, rather than thinking that it may be either and that we do not know to which category to assign it (see ARGUMENT FROM IGNORANCE). Or it may be that a proposition is simply neither true nor untrue, but, say, emotive. Nietzsche has suggested that the categories true and false have no inherent meaning but are instead social signals that define a particular power structure. In any case rhetoricians must be constantly on the alert for such binary divisions in their own writing and the writing of others (to use, immediately, a binary division). Also see EQUIVOCATION. Again let me stress that the use of the either/or argument is widespread and, further, that in its most frequently found form, it involves the problem of definition in at least one of its terms (hence the caution to see EQUIVOCATION). Also see, for a related discussion, DISJUNCTIVE SYLLOGISM, with the caution that the rules of validity in the syllogistic form evade the preceding problems.

The antithesis of the either/or, is, of course, the much less frequently encountered "both/and," skillful use of which can sometimes counter the divisive intent of the either/or. The idea is essential, for instance, to the concept of "diversity" and "multiculturalism" proposed as social virtues.

ELLIPSIS
An ellipsis is a deliberate omission formally marked in American typography by three or more spaced periods. It

has two basic functions. When it is employed in a quotation, it constitutes an acknowledgment that what is presented is not the totality of the statement and that the reader who wishes to may consult the original to assure herself that the omission does not change or distort its meaning. When it is employed outside of a quotation, it signals something like the expression "Well, I guess I don't need to go on. You get the picture." It represents, when so used, a choice not to specifically state the content that the reader presumably can fill in for herself. It allows that reader to fill the blank with whatever she is most comfortable with and can thus function to bring the reader into the argument in a participatory way.

EMOTION

The term *emotional* is often used in opposition to *logical*, implying that the logical is to be preferred (see EITHER/OR). It is frequently implied that it is possible, even desirable, to conduct communication in some mode that is *only* logical. The character of Mr. Spock has been treated as a sort of continuous commentary on the comic possibilities of such a state. While others look frantically for some alternative to seemingly certain annihilation, Mr. Spock finds (logically) some aspect of the prospect merely "interesting" (which in itself constitutes an emotional response–there is no "logical" reason why any one thing should be more interesting than any other). Symbolic logic is, in part, an attempt to strip ordinary language arguments of their ambiguity and emotional baggage and to render them in terms similar to those used in mathematics. Whether or not that attempt can succeed, as rhetoricians we need to be clear that there is "logic" and that there are "logics," and insofar as we have made a systematic study of any area, emotion included, we have consistently found some sort of "logic," some "system" of organization. Hence it is simplistic to categorize an argument as "emotional," whether one intends to therefore, dismiss it or not. Although it is problematic, it is standard practice to talk about *degrees* of emotion (i.e., "highly emotional," etc.). No matter how hard the writer might try to avoid it, there is a content to any statement that is or is not accepted by the reader or hearer on bases prior to *any* possible application of logic. To attempt to dismiss an argument on the basis that it is "emotional" implies that the argument could be otherwise or could, at least, be *less* emotional. Yet even if this were possible, it remains true that all arguments begin with a set of premises that have been accepted on "faith," or as "givens," or as SURDS, or even "emotionally." See LOGIC.

ENDORSEMENT

To endorse something is to "put one's name to it" in some sense, to declare support for and approval of the item endorsed. The hoped-for effect of the endorsement is that those qualities associated with the endorser will be associated with the item endorsed. In all rhetorical forms (advertising being one), the endorsement is a powerful tool and at least as problematic in its application as the *ad hominem* argument, of which it is the reverse. Although it is not often so thought of, "endorsement" is involved when one writer or thinker invokes another by quoting from her or by "dropping" her name in association with something being put forward. Endorsements can come from individuals and from groups (Hakeem Olajuwon and the American Civil Liberties Union) and be of products, persons, institutions, or positions (scotch whiskey, Lee Brown, Bay Manor Hotel, or pro-choice).

ENTHYMEME   (*EN* THUH MEEM)

An enthymeme is a SYLLOGISM in which one premise is IM-PLICIT. Often an enthymeme is used in argument to avoid calling attention to the weakness of the implicit premise. Most arguments are presented as enthymemes, which is to say in most arguments one of the premises is unstated, usually because it is assumed to be so obvious as to be un-needed. If we assume that the SYLLOGISM is the form basic to logic and that the enthymeme is the form in which it most often appears in both written and spoken argument, careful reconstruction of enthymemic presentations is of-ten useful to the rhetorical analyst. One might say, for in-stance, in response to some quasi-religious reference to the greatness of Socrates, "Socrates is dead." The implied conclusion here is that, on the basis of the unstated prem-ise "Things that die are mortal," Socrates is therefore mor-tal. Implicit in *this* is a historical reference to the statement in the famous syllogism that Socrates is "a man" (i.e., "only" human) and that reverential invocations of the So-cratic are thus mistaken. (The full classical statement of the syllogism is "All men are mortal. Socrates is a man. Therefore Socrates is mortal.")

EPIPHANY

An epiphany is a "vision" that presumably comes from wherever it is held that "truth" resides (i.e., from God or some heavenly messenger, or from the recesses of the un-derstanding as accessed through meditation, etc.). The content of the epiphany is thus given the infallibility of the source, held to constitute true "knowledge." Because any-one can make an epiphanic claim, the strength of the claim most frequently depends on the *ETHOS* of the claimant. Think, for instance, of how claims to a "vision" would be received if they were made by the Dalai Lama, and then another set were made by Timothy McVeigh. Consider further, however, claims made by David Koresh and those that presumably inspired the suicides in the Heaven's Gate cult.

In terms of intended intensity, one might consider APERÇU as the weakest form in the series *aperçu, insight, vision, epiphany, revelation*. The last three of these terms are most frequently associated with religious truth claims of one kind or another.

In anything that can be considered an intellectual life, or, perhaps in any life in which there are formulaic responses, there will be a series of what might be called "revelation" points, the kind of forehead-slapping, "of course" acceptances that are so obvious when they occur—and from which the poverty, the sheer inadequacy of the previous position is made clear—that those moments of "revelation" are difficult to identify, date, or isolate for the simple reason that the recipient would not like to confess, even to herself, that she had, theretofore, been ignorant of the revelation. These are the moments that can be referred to as "epiphanic."

EPISTEMOLOGY

Epistemology is that branch of philosophy (the seeking of wisdom) that deals with the area of *how* we know (which, of course, begs the question of whether we really know anything at all—which leads to the famous Socratic "He alone is wise who knows he knows nothing"). So-called "cognitive science," which investigates actual physical responses in the brain to various stimuli (as, for instance, in language acquisition), may be thought of as philosophy's current approach to the epistemic problem.

EPITHET

Epithet has two nearly opposite meanings, the most frequently used of which is an offensive or insulting term for an individual or a group (see FEAR, APPEAL TO). The other meaning is a term that attaches to an individual or group as an honorific: "the Great Communicator" (Reagan), "The Great Emancipator" (Lincoln), the "Bard" (Shakespeare), "the King" (Presley), "the Glimmer Twins" (Jagger and Richards), but not "Tricky Dick" (Nixon) or "Slick Willie" (Clinton).

EQUIVOCATION

Equivocation is always involved with DEFINITION in that she who equivocates uses a word *in two or more senses* without distinguishing between or among them. A classic example is the mock-syllogism "Some dogs have spots. My dog has spots. Therefore my dog is some dog!" A more subtle example is James Baker's reply–to the question about his party dumping Dan Quayle before George Bush ran for his second term as president–that such an option "was never seriously discussed or considered." The key equivocal word here is "seriously." Consider also in this regard the intended effect of the "or" between "discussed" and "considered." So also equivocation is involved in a syllogism such as "Red is pretty. That dress is red. Therefore that dress is pretty." At first glance this looks like the fallacy of the undistributed middle (see DISTRIBUTION). When it is considered more closely, however, we see that the statement says that "red" is pretty. It does not say that red things are pretty. Often equivocal statements involve the either/or problem by implication. The earlier example of the GM stock (see *AD HOMINEM* CIRCUMSTANTIAL) gives an instance of this. The statement is that GM "is or is not" a good stock. By implication, if GM "is not" a good stock, one could argue that it is therefore a "bad" stock. The equivocation here involves the assumption that "not good" automatically means "bad" or, more specifically, the speaker's wishing the audience to draw that inference. The question is complex, but it is the very complexity of it that often allows the equivocation to escape unnoticed. What is undefined here is "good *for what?*" If we mean that GM stock is not good for people, say, in high-income tax brackets, then it definitely *does not* follow that GM being "not good" implies that it is bad.

ERGO   (*UR* GO OR *AIR* GO)

Ergo is the Latin term for "therefore," "hence," "consequently," "it follows that. . . ." It is often used to give an air of formality to a presentation of the conclusion to an argument. Like the less frequently used *Q.E.D.*, it implies that the person presenting the argument is "learned" or specifically trained in logic.

ETHOS   (*EE* THAS OR *EE* THOWS)

Ethos is a rhetorical term used to mean "character," in the sense that we use that term in the phrase "character reference" (always favorable). Typically a writer attempts to establish her *ethos* (good "character") in specific relationship to the intended audience. The descriptions of particular instances are many. Among them, for instance, are:

> person of extensive education and serious thought,
> person of little formal education but great wisdom,
> tough guy who is a heavy thinker, and
> woman of wit and social concern.

Ethos and attempts to establish it are always of concern to the rhetorician because of its relationship to credibility (see AUTHORITY and PERSONA). *Ethos* and "authority" are always related. Some of the most powerful tools used in the construction of *ethos* are references to authority, presumably derived from education and experience ("As a doctor, I have had contact with hundreds of people who . . ."). *Ethos* is the third of the three basic rhetorical forms in Aristotle, the other two of which are *Pathos* and *Logos*. See *PATHOS,* VOICE, and TONE.

ETYMOLOGY, ARGUMENT FROM   (ET UH *MOLL* UH GEE)

There are many variations on the argument from etymology, but most of them work on the assumption that an "earlier" meaning of a word is somehow closer to what a word "really" means. Current lexicography and, as mentioned earlier, the principle on which the massive authority of the *Oxford English Dictionary* is based are, however, most simply that the definition of a word can be derived *only* from current use. This does not mean that etymology is not a worthwhile subject of investigation, nor that it has nothing to contribute to argument. It means only that any argument based on what a word "really" means has no substance. All "meaning" is derived from use. See DICTIONARY.

EUPHEMISM   (*YOU* FEM ISM)

As popularly understood, a euphemism is a supposedly less offensive word substituted for one that is (or is potentially) offensive. The often-given example is the "substitution" of "passed on" for "died." To label this a euphemism, however, implies that the "real" fact of the matter is that someone is dead and the user of the so-called euphemism either doesn't want to face that fact or wants to postpone facing it.

Consider, however, that what is implied by preferring one use to the other is a whole system of belief concerning the limitations of human mortality. Hence the question to be reckoned with in deciding whether a given structure is or is not a euphemism is "*Is* this a 'substitution,' or is a different attitude expressed?" At the basis of the question is the naive attitude that things have "real" names and that the use of any other term than the "real" one constitutes an evasion of the "true nature" of the item in question.

EVALUATIVE
A word that is "evaluative" carries with it a value judgment, but the reader cannot always tell if a given word in a given piece of writing is to be so classified. A term that was at one time considered to be descriptive may, depending on the particular political climate, become evaluative. "Savage," for instance, is now no longer used to describe a member of a population of aboriginals, but has become a highly negative adjective. Although we no longer have "savages," we still have "savage attacks." The term *primitive* is similarly considered suspect when it is applied to a people rather than to a tool in its earliest stage of development. The word *bastard* may be, depending on the circumstances, an insult ("We've had enough bastards trying to run this place") or a simple descriptive ("Woody Allen's bastard son"). Here again the analyst needs to be careful about assuming that a writer intends a given term as descriptive or evaluative. This is particularly problematic when the argument being analyzed is not contemporary. The term *noble savage,* for instance, could be used without any ironic intention in the eighteenth and nineteenth centuries. See LOADED DICTION.

EVIDENCE

Evidence is information offered in support of a given position and thus frequently constitutes part of an argument. However, the fact that a writer offers evidence or, as it is more commonly put, "backs up" her assertion, does not in and of itself mean that the evidence is sufficient or that the argument is SOUND. To make this determination the reader is obliged to evaluate the evidence in terms of its relevance and sufficiency. This is part of the process involved in the metaphoric expression "weighing the evidence," which can be taken to imply considering not only the amount of evidence but also how well it balances against information that could be considered as counterevidence.

EXAGGERATION

The technical rhetorical term for *exaggeration* is *hyperbole*. To exaggerate is to misrepresent by overstating. This misrepresentation, however, may be a deliberate device that depends for effect on its being recognized as such (see IRONY) and as such is recognized as a legitimate means of emphasis.

EXISTENTIAL IMPORT

A coinage, a NEOLOGISM through use, often gains existential import. The concept is related to the thinking that underlies what is called "reification." If, for example, the words "creation science" are said and written together often enough, the phrase *may* come to be accepted as meaningful. At the moment the combination is most frequently taken to be oxymoronic. "Creation," in this context, assumes a *divine* creator who performs a "miracle." "Science," as we currently understand it and certainly as it is defined within its own DOMAIN, seeks explanation for phenomena from *empirical* data. The "miraculous," within a religious domain, is precisely that which (it is argued) *cannot* be empirically explained. Hence "creation science" is self-contradictory or depends on a definition of "science" that the discipline itself would reject. What is at issue here is a hierarchy of domains. Scientists would claim that using what they see as "their" term ("science") alongside "creation," which they would see as a term that depends on the argument from IGNORANCE, subverts science education by PRIVILEGING religion.

It has been argued that *any* ABSTRACTION, if it is to become meaningful, must go through the process of gaining existential import. In *1984* George Orwell argues that ideas can be eliminated from consciousness by eliminating the words used to invoke the ideas. Orwell's claim is that if one doesn't have a *word* for a concept, one cannot have the concept. Imagine, for instance, asking an aborigine who believes she is told how to behave by the spirit of an eagle that speaks to her directly to be "reasonable." Since (at least) the fifth century BCE, "reasonableness" has been a concept, an *abstraction,* upon which the Western world has placed a great deal of emphasis. It is feasible to say that for the aborigine the word *reason* has no meaning *without* saying, or implying, that the aborigine *has not yet discovered* what the word *reason* means (i.e., without saying that the aborigine is ignorant). Rather, one can say that for the aborigine, the word *reason* lacks existential import. See REASON and REIFY.

EXPLICIT
Explicit is perhaps best understood rhetorically as that which is distinct from the *IMPLICIT.* The explicit states directly as opposed to indirectly.

EXPOSITION

Exposition, or expository writing, is traditionally understood as writing that aims to *transmit* information to presumably interested parties as distinguished from writing that aims to *persuade* the reader. As there will be elements of persuasive writing in expository, so also will there be elements of the expository in persuasive.

In the following discussion, however, the perspective is that of rhetorical analysis, which regards *all* written communication (including the note on the refrigerator door) as guided by a communicative/persuasive purpose. Exposition is, then, that type of prose writing that *attempts* to create, in its target audience, the attitude that the writer is OBJECTIVELY presenting the FACTS relevant to a given subject. Exposition thus is not a division of prose discourse according to intent, but rather represents a tone that the writer wishes the reader to accept as "factual." The writer of exposition cultivates a tone designed to allow (encourage) the reader to think that the writer has no specific interest in, or position in regard to, the subject matter presented. See PERSUASIVE WRITING.

EYE DIALECT

See DIALECT. Eye dialect is a manner of written presentation intended to suggest regional, racial, or ethnic pronunciations particularly when those pronunciations might be simply the way a given word would be read aloud in a particular region or by a particular group (writing *darling* as *darlin'*, for instance). The Texan Molly Ivins frequently writes "Miz" to invoke the pronunciation characteristic of her region, regardless of the fact that many of her readers would so pronounce "Mrs." anyway and perhaps because "Ms" (which is pronounced "Miz") does not invoke the ambiance she wishes.

FACT

That there is such a thing as a "fact" is a subject of some philosophical dispute. Outside of a TAUTOLOGY, can we say that there is such a thing as a "factual" statement about the world? We often use the term *fact* when we should properly use *assertion*. So, when an individual or corporation states something like "Bayer, the aspirin of choice for three out of four Americans," our question might be "Can this assertion be verified?" If it can, and it is, at that point it becomes a "fact." The question of whether it is "really" a fact then involves what we are willing to accept as verification and our rigor in pursuing that verification. Typically we would expect to rely on records, but records, as we know, can be falsified. And we have the further complications of information being gathered by survey, which survey is usually constructed by people employed by parties with a financial interest in the outcome of the survey.

Obviously we cannot, and do not, verify everything that is presented to us as a fact, but as rhetoricians we should at least ask two questions concerning such presentations: (1) is this assertion even *potentially* verifiable? And if it is, (2) does it seem to be in accord with the best information we have for testing it? Even then, we should remain ultimately dubious, but act from some position like "Although this assertion has not been ultimately demonstrated, I am willing to accept it as 'factual' for the moment and at least until the appearance of some contrary claim or evidence." The large problem comes when we try to move from fact to meaning—as, for instance, in the statement "The facts speak for themselves." In logic and rhetoric, the facts *never* speak for themselves. They must first be put inside of some theory, which "fact" is demonstrated by the "fact" that *what* "facts" speak for themselves must be distinguished from other so-called "irrelevant" facts (hence it is the *theory* that tells us *which* facts we select to "speak for themselves"). In the aspirin example, we might well imagine that statement followed by "The facts speak for themselves." Consider what we are being asked to infer from this—presumably that Bayer aspirin is therefore the "best." "Best" *for what?* And *for whom?* "Best" for the money? (Presumably the cost of an item has some relation to its sales success.) Do Asians and Europeans take Bayer in such proportions? Will the statement still be accurate (if it is) after the next sales quarter? In how many markets is it the only aspirin available? (Pepsi drinkers, for instance, are currently out of luck if they fly Southwest Airlines.) And so forth.

The point is that the "fact" (if it is a fact) does *not* speak for itself. We must bring a large number of (in this case naive) assumptions to it before it will "speak." It is not a "fact," for instance, that smoking causes cancer. There is, however, a *very high statistical probability, given the factors that have been examined,* that it does. Notice also here how the "fact" of the matter is rendered conditional by the language in which the statement is cast. What does "the aspirin of choice" mean? Might it indicate, because the chemical content of *all* aspirin is the same, that Bayer has a higher name recognition than, say, Walgreen aspirin? What kind of choice were *what* Americans given to elicit this answer?

To take another example, consider the apparently simple, apparently "factual" statement "Sam shot Bill." Let us say it is ballistically demonstrable that the slug entering Bill's skull in the presence of an eyewitness issued from a revolver in Sam's hand and that the eyewitness further saw Sam's finger pull the trigger on that revolver that was pointed at Bill, heard the report of the exploding shell, saw a hole appear in Bill's forehead, and saw Bill fall. Further let us say that this shooting took place in a locked bank vault and that only Sam, Bill, and the eyewitness were present, although the whole event was taped on the security monitors. Let us further assume that the tape was not tampered with and (for purposes of the argument) *that the eyewitness tells the truth.* Surely we can say that the statement "Sam shot Bill" is a fact.

What, however, can we say that this "fact" says? Can we take the statement "Sam shot Bill," for instance, as the equivalent of the statement "Sam is responsible for Bill's death"? What do the "facts" tell us? What, in other words, do the facts "speak for"? Was Sam awake? Did he know that the gun was loaded? Was Sam in a hypnotic state? Did Sam intend to miss Bill but instead hit him by accident?

FACTS, THE

On the radio and then television series *Dragnet,* Sergeant Friday (L.A.P.D.) would, sooner or later, interrupt a witness he and his partner were questioning with the (flat, "emotionless") phrase "Just the facts, Ma'am." The witness would pause, try to figure out what Friday meant, and then usually provide what he was looking for. What Friday meant by "the facts" was those data that would support the hypothesis that he was professionally dedicated to—that a crime had been committed. The witness, who was usually just trying to figure out what had happened, inevitably had to adjust her selection of narrative detail to corroborate that hypothesis. *All data are facts,* but "*the* facts" are those data that a particular hypothesis (such as, in this case, that a crime has been committed) depends on. We often encounter an expression from some official or another to the effect that "I would rather not make any statements until all the facts are in." What "*the* facts" are, and how one tells them from other data, is determined by what one is looking for. The theory, thus, comes first and constitutes a filter that determines which facts are relevant. The same principle applies when we encounter the phrase "The *fact* is. . . ." What the rhetorician needs to look at in these cases is not so much the "facts" but what thesis these bits of data are being used to support.

FAITH

The word *faith* has religious associations that, for many, would make it inappropriate for a rhetorical discussion. Nevertheless, faith is the point from which all arguments, if taken from their initial terms, begin. Neither LOGIC nor REASON has a *content* as such. Rather, the first is a name for a series of rules for dealing systematically with assertions, and the second is the name of a supposed mental faculty that permits that dealing. The *source* of those assertions, *ultimately,* is antecedent to the exercise of this faculty and these rules. When Thomas Jefferson wrote, "We hold these truths to be self evident . . ." he was asserting a belief ostensibly shared by a specific and revolutionary group (see TRUTH). The wording "we *hold*" implies "we take it as an item of faith—as a point *outside of and prior to* argument." Monarchists, British or not, certainly did not "hold" that "all men are created equal." Indeed, the statement is contrary to what simple observation would seem to reinforce—equality, if *observable* at all, is among the last qualities that would be noted and would certainly depend upon a fairly sophisticated definition of that term. What, then, can be the authority for Jefferson's statement? There is none, as he well knows. Hence the "we hold" part of the phrase. He says, with this, that the statement itself is the central item of "our" faith (we *now, with this declaration,* non-British, we would-be *Americans*). He says this further as an "enlightenment" thinker, as a prime representative of the "age of reason," the supposed dawning of the emergence from the "dark ages" of superstition and "belief." Gary Wills in his Pulitzer Prize-winning *Lincoln at Gettysburg* argues that Lincoln, in the "Gettysburg Address," makes, *without argument,* into an item of faith what Jefferson's audience would *not* accept— that Jefferson's phrase "all men" included blacks. Given that the North won the war, Lincoln's *reading* of Jefferson's statement has been untouchable. Whatever the personal attitude of the particular legislator, it would be well nigh impossible to assert that the authors of the Declaration of Independence did not *mean* to include black people.

Rhetorically considered, then, *faith* is here defined as that which ultimately underlies all processes of reasoning. One reasons *from* principles. The source of those principles, by definition, is prior to reason (one must reason, if one can discover the points of origin, *from* some set of premises, which is not derived from reason).

Belief, a less religiously charged word for what is held on faith, might be considered as a substitute. If X is *demonstrable,* one does not need to say, "I believe X." One can instead say, "X is the case because of A and B." In the same way, one does not need to have faith in that which is evident. However, unlike the case with the term *faith,* when "belief" is invoked in an argument, what is usually involved is an *AD POPULUM* APPEAL. Bertrand Russell famously defined *belief* as "an idea or image combined with a yes-feeling."

As is the case with Jefferson, a sense of "we" is invoked, and that "we" is inevitably a "we" opposed to some "they," some set of nonbelievers, of "infidels."

See SURD.

FALLACY

The term *fallacy* is frequently used to mean "a commonly held but erroneous belief." Someone, for instance, might say, "Eskimos have three hundred different words for *snow*." We would not be surprised by someone else replying, "That's a fallacy. Basically they have only four words for *snow*." From the perspective of rhetorical analysis, however, such usage constitutes an "error" or a "mistake," but not a fallacy. A fallacy, within the domains of logic and rhetoric, is that which violates the accepted standards of VALID argument, which simply presenting incorrect information does not do.

Note, however, that to show that an argument is fallacious is *not* a demonstration of the falseness of its conclusion. If an argument is fallacious, the conclusion may be either true or false, but it is *not* demonstrated to be true from the argument in question. That an argument is not true for X reason does not imply that it may not be true for Y reason. That all dogs are named Spot, and this animal is a dog (the first premise is obviously false, and, in the circumstances, the second premise is false as well in that the animal referred to just happens to be a cat) does not mean that the conclusion "Therefore this animal is named Spot" (which conclusion taken with the premises constitutes a valid syllogism) is false. Nor does it mean it is true. The animal referred to is, or is not, named Spot, no matter what argument is brought to bear about it. This strictly logical usage of the term is sometimes distinguished from what are called the INFORMAL FALLACIES. See FALSE.

FALSE

It is important not to confuse the meanings of *false* and *invalid*. A conclusion may not follow from the premises used to support it and hence be an "invalid conclusion," yet still be true. It can also be a valid conclusion and be false. Let us say that Rover is a dog. Take the following syllogism: "All blue things are dogs. Rover is a blue thing. Therefore Rover is a dog." Both premises are false, the syllogism is valid, and the conclusion is true. Try then this syllogism: "All dogs are gray. Rover is blue. Therefore Rover is a dog." The premises are both false, and the syllogism is invalid. The conclusion, nevertheless, is true. Generally, and loosely, we may assume that *false* means contrary to the truth, which, of course, involves us in that fun question "What is the truth?" See TRUTH and VALID.

FEAR, APPEAL TO

See *AD BACULUM.* From one perspective the appeal to fear details how the argument from force is intended to operate. That my revolver and pair of tens beats your three queens depends on your fear of my shooting you if you do not allow me to take the pot. Hence I did not "really" win, I only picked up the pot, which, given sufficient firepower, I could have done without even having been a player. In the appeal to fear, the "other" and/or the unknown are the equivalent of the gun. "I'm gonna tell Momma" and "Wait until your father gets home" are both appeals to this "other," the absent figure who is presumed to represent the force parallel to the revolver's.

In writing, however, such an appeal may not be as obvious. Suggesting, for instance, that Queer Nation (a politically active homosexual organization) has designs on your children (presuming that you are straight) is an appeal to fear. It depends on a response that assumes that homosexuality and, by extension, sympathy for or membership in any other "other" group (radicals, communists, liberals, gays, blacks, whites, Asians, Hispanics, Jews, Catholics, Muslims) represent, *from the perspective of the group representing itself as threatened*, a loss of those values that constitute normalcy and decency (see *AD POPULUM*). The names just given, of course, are *not* those that an argument from fear would use (except that liberals, interestingly, remain "liberals," with the likely preface of "Goddamned"). The others become, point to point, "terrorists," "commies" or "reds," "fags" or "queers," "niggers," "whitey" or "honkies," "slopes" or "Japs" or "Chinks," "greasers" or "spics," "kikes," "snappers," and "Arabs" (usually pronounced "A-rabs").

It may not be immediately apparent that the use of these epithets automatically implies the argument from fear, but consider that in each case not only is the supposedly neutral appellation for the group avoided but also in each case *membership in the group is assumed to define the most constitutive aspect of any individual member thereof.* Fear and hatred, from the perspective of the argument offered, are near-allied. The rhetor who employs the argument from fear attempts to invoke that fear through expressions consonant with hatred. Further, when this fear is invoked, it is invoked in the name of some supposed institution like "the American way of life" or "family values" or "the Western tradition" and so forth.

The Mafia, the Masons, the Knights of Columbus, the Ku Klux Klan, fraternities and sororities, and street gangs are all designed to secure exclusive benefits for their members. For this, the membership–brothers or sisters, family, or however designated–owes its first loyalty to other members and the leadership of the group. Any outsider is understood as constituting a potential threat to the privileged status of the members.

The outsider, the "other," has been a central aspect of the history of peoples and of nations for as long as these abstractions ("peoples" and "nations") have existed. The term *barbarian,* which we now understand to refer to one who is unmannered, crude, and cruel, meant originally "non-Greek" and included everyone who was not a citizen of Greece. *Goyim* doesn't mean Catholic, or even Christian, but non-Jewish. *Gajin* does not mean Westerner, or Occidental, but rather non-Japanese. This is to say that outside of whatever group we are discussing stands only one entity, a faceless totality that constitutes the "other."

Dr. Johnson, in his 1755 *Dictionary of the English Language,* defines *patriotism* as the last resort of the scoundrel, his point being that if one tries to induce action by an appeal to patriotism it constitutes an appeal of the last resort and indicates lack of any other, or any sufficient, argument. From this perspective, all requests for loyalty and all appeals to patriotism depend on the "other" constituting a threat to the benefits available to group members. Such appeals—depending, of course, as always on the target audience—can be very powerful. An appeal that asks for loyalty, therefore, as the appeal based on patriotism, must issue from somewhere, and the rhetor needs to ask, in her analysis, whose purposes will be served by response to the appeal. The principle is the same whether one is being asked to be "true to" one's family, one's school, one's city, one's state, one's country, one's gender, one's race, or one's religion. Each of these is an abstraction, and none of them, in the final analysis, has any existence outside of its membership.

It is not difficult to make the case that appeals to patriotism and loyalty are invoked in the face of a threat. What is less clear is that appeals to "progress," "the future," and "our "destiny," although not overtly defensive, remain appeals to fear. If I argue that the "Aryan peoples" need room to fulfill their destiny or argue that "manifest destiny" excuses displacing the native population, in urging these things I am appealing to fear. If, that is, the Aryan peoples do *not* secure *lebensraum,* the implication is that they will not only not fulfill their glorious promise but also that they will die. If the "manifest destiny" of the former colonists is not fulfilled, they will be weak and vulnerable.

FIGURE OF SPEECH

A figure of speech is a nonliteral linguistic construction such as a metaphor. To say that someone is as happy as a lark, or down in the dumps, or bored out of her skull is to use a "figure" of speech. Language that is "figured" or "figurative" is usually distinguished from "plain" speech or writing, although a little thought reveals that the expression "plain speech" is, in itself, figurative. The problem is in the nature of metaphor, which is so pervasive an aspect of language as to be, for all intents and purposes, "inescapable" (to use a figure of speech). See METAPHOR and especially TROPE. See also LITERALLY and CLICHÉ.

FOLK SAYING

A folk saying is a form of adage (see APHORISM) attributed to a group of people usually characterized by little formal education and low income (the "common" people) who, because they are not subject to the distortions of "reality" (with which reality "the folk" are taken to be in contact) that sophisticated (or *un*common) people experience, are a repository of wisdom. To repeat a folk saying as support for one's argument is thus a form of ARGUMENT FROM AUTHORITY in that the folk, like children (see INNOCENCE, ARGUMENT FROM), are held to be in direct contact with "real life." Folk sayings are as liable to error as any other statement, and the rhetorician considering their invocation needs, as always, to be conscious of the predilections of the TARGET AUDIENCE.

FORCED HYPOTHESIS

To call a conclusion to an argument a "forced hypothesis" makes no specific claim against the argument but asserts, simply, that the conclusion drawn does not follow from the arguments presented. The term is so general that we can only assume that it means that the person using it has not been convinced by the argument she is so labeling. Simply put, one can refer to any argument with which one does not agree as a "forced hypothesis." See *NON SEQUITUR*.

GENDER

Current EDUCATED USAGE defines one's "gender" as one's membership in a sex-based category that is defined socially. One's "sex," however, is defined biologically. Hence what I refer to as a "gender-identifiable pronoun" (*he* or *she*, as opposed to *they*) presumes not a biological difference between the beings referred to, but rather a social difference. If you (see DIRECT ADDRESS) have been annoyed with this book's use of the female pronoun where the male is traditional, you are in some way responding to the social categorization.

GIVEN

To treat a statement as a "given" is to agree to suspend any reservations concerning its acceptability until some undetermined time (which may never occur). The "given" is that which is "taken for granted," and "taking for granted" always involves an implicit hypothetical. "Taking for granted X, we can understand Y" is, in other words, implicitly equivalent to the more clearly hypothetical "*If* we take X for granted, then we can understand Y." See TRUTH CLAIM and ACCOMMODATORS.

HARD COPY

Hard copy is computer terminology and distinguishes between the printed page and its electronic form, whether as WYSIWYG pixels on a monitor or in bit form storage. I may use e-mail or the Web to transmit written material, but it is not hard copy until it is printed out. In the discussion at the entry for TEXT, I assert that there are radical differences between the way a reader can react to a text and the way an auditor can react to a speaker. Somewhere between the two of these lies electronic text, and somewhere toward the speaker-auditor end of that continuum lies e-mail. I would suggest that the rhetorical aspects of e-mail are still being formulated. It is too new a medium to have shaken down to what the essential constituents of its rhetorical practice will be.

In relationship to written argument, however, it does show some highly interesting differences from the traditional "reply" or "response" to a position from which a writer differs. It is not possible, practical, or practiced in either speech or text to reply to the whole of the text being commented upon. Instead, points are selected, and quotations are placed only when needed. In the e-mail reply, however, the respondent can simply press "reply" and then in the quotation of the *entire* message, if seen fit, comment at whatever length at any point appropriate (after a single word, or sentence, or paragraph). Given this, subscribers to an online argument have an unparalleled opportunity to agree on what their basic terminology will mean or to recognize early on that no agreement is possible given the way the parties define their terms.

HASTY GENERALIZATION

To label a generalization (to move from a statement about particulars to a statement about the whole) "hasty" is always a judgment call. There is a sense in which any generalization is "hasty" in that it never includes all cases. Hence the charge that a generalization is "hasty" puts the burden of demonstration on the accuser, who must then defend the accusation by presenting a case where the generalization does not hold. Operatively a "hasty" generalization is one that a sophisticated body of thinking persons would so label. See INDUCTIVE ARGUMENT.

HEAT, RHETORICAL

English speakers typically use one of two metaphors to designate the emotional intensity of a given statement: relative hardness and relative temperature. We are told, for instance (and quite accurately), that "the soft answer turneth away wrath." We are told that a position that is unlikely to change has "hardened." In an only slightly MIXED METAPHOR, we are also told that "her words would have melted the hardest of hearts." Presumably this, were metaphoric niceties observed, would be better put as the "coldest" of hearts, but the mixing doesn't stand out because we might remember Pharaoh, who hardened his heart, or Hannah, the hard-hearted, or the failure to free your doubtful mind and melt your cold cold heart. The warm is, for the most part, soft, whereas the colder something is, usually the harder it is. The temperature metaphor is extremely useful to describe the range of emotional intensity of a given expression in that it can be icy, glacial, cold, cool, lukewarm, warm, hot, and even fiery. Consider the relative warmth of the following list of terms.

Shhh
Hush
Shush
Quiet down now
Quiet, please
Please be quiet
Be quiet
Quiet
Silence
Shut up
Shut the f—— up

The list begins at a warmth that could be associated with affection and ends at a heat indicative that the next reaction will be physical rather than verbal.

HEIGHTENED DICTION

Heightened diction describes a choice of words that is deliberately and obviously "above" the merely formal, usually characterized by being alliterative, cadenced, deliberately repetitive, metaphoric (although not all metaphor can be considered "heightened"), "poetic," biblical, inverted (word order), archaic (although still recognizable), or any combination of these. Word choice of this sort is typically used on ceremonial occasions or occasions of high seriousness.

HIDDEN AGENDA

In the entry for DEVIL'S ADVOCATE, I mentioned that a writer could, under the guise of "playing" the devil's advocate, really be advocating the position so presented. To do so would be to have a "hidden" agenda, as well as a "covert" thesis (see THESIS). Foundation reports, or reports from sponsored centers that purport to be "studies" or "investigations" of particular phenomena, are often vehicles for promoting the ideology of the sponsoring organization.

HISTORY, ARGUMENT FROM

The statement "Those who will not learn from history are condemned to repeat it" I hope attests to the use of history as a metonymy or, less specifically, a trope and, I suggest, a major authorizing trope (see TROPE). A multitude of arguments have based themselves on the "lessons" of history, as if history were the name of a single thing. In such invocations "history," whatever that might be, or wherever it might be found, is clearly being privileged not as a theater of discussion but as a source of truth. That is to say that, despite there being no such "thing" as history, the abstraction is treated as a single entity that can be appealed to or consulted concerning the wisdom of certain courses of action. In 1888 De Maupassant described history as "that excitable and lying old lady." Matthew Arnold in 1864 called it "that huge Mississippi of falsehood." What is important to the idea of argument is the privileging of "it."

HOMOIOPTOTON (HOME OY *OP* TUH TAHN)

"If it doesn't fit, you must acquit." Homoioptoton is the repetition of end sounds. It is a kind of playing with rhyme in the hope of making the phrase so rendered memorable. In the Cochran example we have both rhyme and meter (if it DOESn't FIT / you MUST aQUIT) for an apparently winning combination. "Early to bed and early to rise makes a man healthy, wealthy, and wise" illustrates not only rhyme's mnemonic quality but also its association with supposedly "wise" sayings.

HOT-BUTTON

The term *hot-button* is not in the 1991 *OED,* but presumably it derives from Cold War slang and its concerns with "the" button–the nuclear launch button. Like buzz words, most hot-button words go in and out of style fairly quickly or are hot-button words only for particular groups. A hot-button word is one that is intended to produce an immediate and unthinking strong negative response. Here are a few: *fascist, sexist, gang, violence, Nazi, bigot, elitist, crime.* Readers should have no difficulty making up their own lists. Buzz words are intended to make the reader feel impressed; hot-button words are intended to make the reader feel angry.

HYPOCRISY, ACCUSATION OF   (HIP *POCK* RI SEE)

To accuse someone of being a hypocrite is to say that her conduct is not consistent with what she claims to believe. The accusation is always an *ad hominem* argument but is seldom objected to on that basis. That person who is accused of hypocrisy can sometimes claim to be sincere but weak or disadvantaged in some way. Consider, for instance, the parental admonition "Do as I say, not as I do." That is to say, "Because I am going to die of lung disease is no reason for you to adopt my vices." The accusation also functions as a *TU QUOQUE* and as such is not to reply to the claim per se, but to attack the qualifications of the accuser to raise it. See CONSISTENCY.

HYPOTHESIS

Typically the term *hypothesis,* when used as a rhetorical descriptive, is dismissive, as in "That's just a hypothesis." Presumably what happens to "good" hypotheses is that they are tested, preferably "scientifically," and proven to be "true" or "false." Hypotheses when so "proven" presumably become FACTS. The rhetor might consider this statement by the philosopher Peter Caws: "That there is a real world is the best available hypothesis, but it's a hypothesis all the same."

HYPOTHETICAL ARGUMENT

Following are a few of the phrases that are used to introduce hypothetical arguments: "If we begin at X, could we safely say that we will accomplish Y?" "One set of principles we could adopt might look like . . ." "What would happen if we do not accept X?" Logic aside, the usual reason for presenting an argument in the form of a hypothetical or a conditional is to avoid an appearance of rigidity or dogmatism (see HYPOTHETICAL SYLLOGISM). Implied is "What would it hurt to *consider* this? After all, if it doesn't look good, we can reject it." The psychological strategy involved is that once a party to the discussion invests time in a particular consideration, she is (presumably) more *likely* to protect the value of the time invested by accepting the consideration (or some part of it) than to regard the time as necessary in the rejection process. This is why, more often than not (as earlier), the hypothetical is put in the form of a question that implies that anyone who refuses to answer the question is guilty of the ARGUMENT FROM IGNORANCE. Also involved is the "fairness" consideration of "If I am willing to consider your positions, shouldn't you grant me equal time to consider mine, even if only *hypothetically?* What do we have to lose?"

Norman Mailer contributes this metaphoric treatment: "An hypothesis, no matter how uncomfortable or bizarre on its first presentation, will thrive or wither by its ability to explain the facts available." Notice particularly in this regard his phrase "the facts *available.*" Mailer is discussing the theory that Jack Ruby's shooting of Lee Harvey Oswald was a Mafia hit.

HYPOTHETICAL SYLLOGISM

A hypothetical syllogism (see SYLLOGISM) is a set of three statements, one of the first two of which, and sometimes both, contains the "conditional" "if." The following is a "mixed" hypothetical syllogism. Note that it contains one hypothetical and one categorical premise.

> If the dog ate my lunch today, I will go hungry.
> The dog ate my lunch today.
> Therefore, I will go hungry.

In the "pure" hypothetical syllogism both premises are hypothetical.

> If my dog ate my lunch today, he won't bite me.
> If he doesn't bite me, I won't have to get shots.
> Therefore, if my dog ate my lunch today, I won't have to
>   get shots.

These forms, like those of the CATEGORICAL SYLLOGISM, can be useful if one encounters a written argument that can be reduced to them because placing the argument in the appropriate formal statement allows the constituent parts (the "terms"), as well as the relationship that is asserted among those terms, to be clearly seen. Bear in mind, however, that if an argument is changed from its statement in context to the form of a syllogism it can always be argued that the syllogistic form into which it was put does not fit the argument presented.

ICON

An *icon*, as that term applies to written argument, is a simple, easily identifiable graphic (two-dimensional "drawing") that can be a logo very specifically identifiable with a particular group or one more widely symbolic of an attitude or way of thinking. As such it can be considered as closely related to TYPOGRAPHY in argument. A recent example of argument by logo is the bumper sticker that reads "Love is all it takes to make a family" in which the letter "o" in "love" is represented as an equilateral triangle resting on a point, the interior of which is pink. The icon (the pink-filled triangle) is not necessary to the point implicitly argued (that a family need not be composed of at least one male and one female member, but rather needs to be composed only of people who love each other), but it underscores it and a more specific reading applicable to the activist lesbian organization that the logo-become-icon represents. One can think of an icon as a kind of "instant" statement, and as such it is related to other brief forms of presenting positions such as the SOUND BITE and the APHORISM.

IDEOLECT

If a dialect is one of a number of subsets of pronunciations, grammars, vocabularies, and idioms within a given language, an ideolect is a subset of a dialect defined by being the unique combination of these same elements held by an individual. When we become very familiar with a particular writer (say, William F. Buckley or Molly Ivins or even Dave Barry), we can recognize their ideolects in unsigned pieces. An ideolect is what we are talking about when we speak of a writer finding her VOICE. It is that combination of phrasing, rhythm, and vocabulary that stamps a piece of writing as uniquely hers.

IDIOM

Idiom has many meanings, but it may most immediately be understood as a less negatively loaded equivalent for what is called JARGON. One can, for instance, speak of legal jargon or of the legal idiom—it is thus descriptive of a form of language usage particular to a period, a profession, an interest group, or a "school" of activity within a larger grouping (one could speak of a "punk" idiom within a "rock" idiom, for example), or even of the idiom of rhetorical analysis.

An idiom is also, however, an expression that, were the auditor not directly familiar with it, would seem to make no sense. In Texas, for instance, people "swing by," whereas in other parts of the country they might "drop by" or "drop over" or even "drop in."

IGNORANCE, ARGUMENT FROM
This mode of argument is very common and especially pernicious. It involves arguing for the truth of a given statement, a specific conclusion, on the basis of *what we do not know.* To argue that God exists on the grounds that it has never been *disproved* is to argue from ignorance. So also is to argue that there are no such things as elephants because you have never seen one. It is generally granted that one cannot reason to *any* conclusion legitimately on the basis of a claim of ignorance.

IMAGE
This is a very slippery concept in that, strictly speaking, written language (outside of ideograms or pictograms) can no more be imagistic than it can be onomatopoetic–words are not pictures, nor, strictly speaking again, are words on a page *sounds* (at least until they are read aloud). George Orwell, however, has created in "Politics and the English Language" a category for what we might call "language intended to evoke a picture in the mind of the reader." As such, we associate writing that is imagistic with the "concrete" and language that does not, or is not intended to evoke a picture, with the "abstract." See Orwell's essay specifically on all the value judgments associated with such use. See especially ABSTRACT.

IMPLY

That which is implied, which is "implicit," is that which *is not directly stated* but can be "inferred" from what *is* stated. If, for instance, we say that all *A* is *B*, then we can "infer" from that the "implicit" (*not* stated) no *A* is not *B*. Often the writer who relies on implication rather than direct statement is (in Western cultures particularly) seen as devious, even cowardly, in that she appears to be unwilling to take responsibility for a direct statement. She might, for instance, reply to a question of whether she was implying *X* with, "No, I simply stated *Y; you* inferred *X*." The "implication" of this is that the responsibility for the inferred conclusion lies with you, not with the writer, who is hence "not responsible" for "what you made out of it." All irony, for example, works by implication. Utilizing implication rather than direct confrontation, however, is a deliberate and complex rhetorical strategy often seen as advantageous in treating highly inflammatory or divisive topics. See the discussion of the implicit in the entry for THESIS. See ROGERIAN ARGUMENT and ACCOMMODATION.

INDIRECT ARGUMENT

Indirect argument is a literary presentation that avoids the "people who think *X* should think *Y* because of *Z*" appearance of direct persuasion. Its characteristic forms are the PERSONAL ESSAY, the MEDITATION, and the DIALOGUE. Exercises in definition can also be considered a form of indirect argument.

INDUCTIVE ARGUMENT

An inductive argument leads from observations about particular members of a set to an assertion about all members of a set. Hence, unlike DEDUCTIVE ARGUMENT, which moves from the general to the particular, induction moves from the particular to the general. Further, whereas a deductive argument is held to yield truth, the inductive argument yields only likelihood. Induction is the method basic to "scientific experimentation" in that a specified number of repetitions of a given experiment, or the responses of a given *sample* of the population, are held to demonstrate the *probability* that a generalizable principle has been found.

The argument from ANALOGY is sometimes treated as an inductive argument. Inductive arguments are often used in an appeal to pity (see *AD MISERICORDIUM*). The writer will go on in particular detail about the message from the dying mother that didn't go through because the phone was out of order because the father was out of work because federal regulations required a thirty-day waiting period, and so forth. The use of such an ANECDOTE is usually in support of a general change. It might be something like "My pregnant dog was run over, and my invalid mother is heartbroken. Therefore the speed limit on the access road next to my house should be lowered."

INFER, INFERENCE
See IMPLY. The "implication" is the writer's, the "inference" the reader's, or, to put it another way, the writer implies, the reader infers. However, when the word is used in a precise sense in logic, the "inference" is considered to be a part of the statement itself. From the statement "All *A* is *B*," we are logically entitled to "infer" the statement "No *A* is not *B*." Similarly, from "No *A* is *B*" we may infer that "No *B* is *A*."

INFLATED DICTION
One way to think of inflated diction is as HEIGHTENED DICTION that fails. W. C. Fields made a career out of using

inflated diction. He would, for instance, speak of a ponderous pachyderm rather than a large elephant. Fields, of course, aimed at being ridiculous. Most users of inflated diction do not, but rather, by borrowing the devices of heightened diction, intend to lend dignity or high seriousness to their subject. When the opposite is intended, such use is, of course, ironic. When the object of the description "this armored denizen of darkness, this tireless explorer" is a cockroach, one may be *fairly* sure that the writer is being ironic.

INFORMAL FALLACIES

From some perspectives, the term *informal fallacies* is oxymoronic. It is, nevertheless, frequently enough used to require definition here. Irving Copi observes that we use the term most often to refer to arguments that "seem" to be correct but that prove, on closer examination, not to be. Because each of these arguments has its own entry in the glossary, I will only list them here. They fall into two groups. The first are fallacies of "relevance," although, as the individual entries will show, relevance sometimes is a matter of degree rather than an absolute determination. All the glossary entries that begin with the Latin *ad* ("from") fall into this group, to which add POST HOC, ERGO PROPTER HOC; CIRCULAR ARGUMENT; and COMPLEX QUESTION. The second group is composed of what are called fallacies of AMBIGUITY, and the reader is referred to that entry.

INNOCENCE, ARGUMENT FROM

The phrase "out of the mouths of babes" is, like the argument from the folk (see FOLK SAYINGS), an invocation of the idea that civilization takes us away from some construct called "nature," in which dwells "truth." It probably has a lot to do with why we like puppies and kittens and why we recite ANECDOTES of a child or a person who is brain damaged or in some way isolated from the presumably corrupting influences of maturity, who is cited as author of a statement the presenter hopes will be taken as representing a genuine insight. Citations from Native Americans, for instance, participate in this rhetorical endorsement. Implied is something like "Isn't it wonderful that people who did not have indoor plumbing could produce such a wise man as. . . ." Also involved is the notion of the aboriginal as "prior" to the corruption of "civilization" and thus "childlike." See particularly the authorizing trope NATURE, ARGUMENT FROM.

INNOVATION, ARGUMENT FROM

Although it might be argued simply that *innovation*, or *innovative*, is a BUZZ WORD, the buzz would seem to have, by now, attached a clear positive value to the word. Dictionaries, even the hippest, will tell you that an innovation is something new. What they do not say is that the new is assumed to be the "improved." That something is "innovative" is often assumed to be clear evidence that it ought to be applauded, and the word is frequently employed to delay or disarm judgment. It is as if, to reverse the saying, "the old way is the worst way" ("old" being anything prior to the particular "innovation"). The argument from innovation is powerful in an age that sees "discovery" and "new" as automatically implying "progress."

Reflection makes immediately clear that the mere newness of anything is no guarantee of its quality or benefit. It makes clear, as well, that very nearly anything can be called "innovative." In prison reform, for instance, how near are "boot camps" to chain gangs? In the field of teaching, administrators almost uniformly proclaim that "good teaching" should be rewarded and then form committees to seek out "innovative" teaching. "Innovative," in this usage, does not mean that students learn more and retain more; rather it means that the student-teacher ratio is high, the dropout rate is low, and a very high percentage are awarded passing grades. "Distance education" lends an example. Closed-circuit television in the classroom (playing tapes) dates from the late fifties. If the same kind of material is broadcast under the name of distance education, we can call it "innovative teaching."

INSINUATION
Insinuation is a type of *indirect* accusation, sometimes involving what we refer to when we talk about "hinting at" something. Insinuating is closely related to IMPLYING, but most often carries negative associations. When they are not made directly, negatives are usually thought of as insinuated, whereas positives are thought of as implied. This is by no means, however, a hard and fast distinction.

INVALID
See VALID. Although it is often so understood, to determine that an argument is invalid is *not* to say that its conclusion is false. The conclusion may be true, false, or indeterminate, but it is whichever of these it may be *without* relation to the argument. Remember that a conclusion is simply a statement. One can put any number of other statements in front of it (premises) with no effect whatsoever on the truth or falsity of the original statement. In other words, a statement that is true does not become false when it appears as the conclusion to an invalid argument. Consider the following syllogism: "Some people who have read this glossary are blue-eyed. Some blue-eyed people teach English. Therefore some people who have read this document teach English." The conclusion is true, but it is not true because

it follows from the argument, because it does *not* follow from the argument. Let *A* represent "people who have read this glossary." Let *B* represent "blue-eyed people." Let *C* represent "people who teach English." A rendering of the syllogism follows: "Some *A* is *B*. Some *B* is *C*. Therefore some *A* is *C*." The syllogism is invalid. The *conclusion,* however, remains as *true* as it was when it was stated in isolation.

INVECTIVE

Invective is language that directly attacks harshly, coarsely, contemptuously, insultingly. Invective is to be distinguished from SATIRE. NAME-CALLING, at its most abusive, is invective. The rhetorical use of invective is typically an effort to invoke the mentality involved in solidarity rallies, protest meetings, conventions, and so forth. These share the assumption that "we" are the good guys and that "they" are the bad guys and that somehow the worse our side can make their side sound, the more virtuous, by contrast, we are. See PREACHING TO THE CONVERTED and DEMONIZE.

IRONY

Irony has many degrees, but all are variations on the use of a word or phrase intended to be understood as the opposite of what is literally said. Irony can also be an indirect reference to an incongruity. The problem with irony is that the writer must assume that the audience will catch the intention. The person who proposes shooting potential murderers as a way to cut down on homicides *may* be serious, as may have been the author of the Vietnam-era statement "Sometimes you have to destroy a village to save it." It is important to distinguish irony from sarcasm in a *written* as opposed to a spoken text. See SARCASM. To use Socratic irony is to feign ignorance in the manner of Plato's dialogues in which the character Socrates asks questions and pretends ignorance of their answers in order to elicit the desired answer from the other party rather than to simply provide it.

JARGON

Jargon is similar to SLANG in that its use is restricted to a particular group, but typically that group is professional rather than social. A surfer, for instance, would have her "slang," whereas an administrator would have her "jargon." Jargon can be further distinguished from slang in that it is not usually the intention of the user of jargon to exclude outsiders from understanding or to be particularly vivid or original. Writing (or speech) that contains a great deal of slang constitutes an "argot," while writing that contains a great deal of jargon is known as "lingo." When the word *jargon* is used in a pejorative sense, it is typically meant that the user of jargon is failing to communicate because she is outside of her group or that she is intentionally either obscuring or inflating the importance of whatever she is referring to. Jargon is not to be confused with "technical" language that, although it may not be widely *understandable,* is nevertheless commonly *available* in appropriate dictionaries. A physician may, for instance, refer to the "second intercostal space" (between the first and second ribs) without using jargon. See IDIOM.

KAIROS

Kairos is a term from classical rhetoric that is enjoying a revival in contemporary rhetorical theory. Its primary application is to oratory. Isocrates defines it as "fitness for the occasion." The considerations are so complex that I have chosen to discuss them under a number of different heads, central of which is TARGET AUDIENCE. See also DISCOURSE COMMUNITY.

KILL THE MESSENGER
The absolute ruler, having received bad news, expresses her anger by having the bringer of the news put to death. This may have a couple of effects, at least one of which will be to discourage the carrying of bad news. Baldly stated, the concept looks silly, but it is with us in many forms and operates in nearly all areas of argument, usually in ways that can be discussed as *AD HOMINEM.* In an anecdote from the practice of courtroom law, a young lawyer asks a more experienced lawyer: "In that we have no defense whatsoever, what am I to do?" The reply is, "Abuse plaintiff," which should tell us why the *ad hominem* is sometimes referred to as *ad hominem, abusive.* The strategic point is to distract attention from the accusation being brought by attacking the bringer of the accusation.

LADDER OF ABSTRACTION, THE
See ABSTRACTION. The linguist (and later U.S. senator) S. I. Hayakawa originated this concept as a way of dealing with levels of abstraction in their relationship to communication. At the *most* concrete level of specificity where there would be the *least* amount of confusion, instead of saying "this" and pointing, one would physically put one's hand on whatever was being referred to. Conversation, at this level, would be impossible because one could talk only about what one could touch (Fido, but not *dogs*). Jonathan Swift in *Gulliver's Travels* has the philosophers of Laputa communicate by taking objects out of bags they carry on their backs and setting the objects down between them. A "reply" to one object would be another object. A particular ladder might run, for instance, (from most abstract to

least) from everything to everything living, everything living and four-legged, living four-legged and domestic, and bovine, and belonging to farmer Brown, and in farmer Brown's southeast pasture, northeast corner, that cow, Bossy. Hayakawa suggests that discourse takes place as high on the ladder as is possible until some confusion occurs. At that point the conversants descend the ladder until the confusion disappears (with, for instance, an "example," which is a *specific* illustration of a more abstract concept). "Give me an example" is a request for the speaker to drop down the ladder temporarily until clarity is reestablished. In written argument the level of abstraction is particularly problematic because the writer has no way of checking in with her audience to see if her chosen level is too high for clarity.

LEXICON

A lexicon is a collection, or stock, of words. This stock may be characteristic of an individual, a profession, a philosophy, or a "style" (such as, say, a sermon), or it may be as unrestricted as an unabridged dictionary. A lexicon is usually to be distinguished from a glossary in being less focused and less restrictive. It could be argued, for instance, that this glossary need not, even ought not, contain the word *lexicon* in that, as is the case with many of the words discussed here, it is not a word with a special meaning within the analysis of rhetoric. I would respond that insofar as it is a word used to describe the range of vocabulary from which a given discipline or individual chooses, it is a word that can be useful to the rhetor. See ARGOT.

LITERALLY

Literally has both a strict and a common use. In the strict use it means the opposite of *figuratively* or *metaphorically*. If one says that an opera singer's performance "brought the house down," *figuratively* it would mean that she was hugely applauded. *Literally* it would mean that the opera house collapsed. In common use *literally* is an intensifier, something like "really," as in "they really applauded hard." A rhetorician would use the word in its strict sense to emphasize that what might sound like a metaphoric or figurative description is instead (or additionally) accurate and precise.

LOADED DICTION

Loaded diction is a subtle type of NAME-CALLING that involves selecting words to describe a particular thing, which words either elevate (if positively loaded) or denigrate (if negatively loaded) that thing. Like the more obvious forms of name-calling, it is not an argument but rather an attempt to influence an audience's judgment by invoking an ARGUMENT FROM ASSOCIATION. An essay titled "TV Can't Educate" refers to a particular newscaster's "studied casual manner." If one practices (studies) being casual long enough, one may become casual. In which case one's manner *is* casual. If one studies enough to *act* casual, but fails to *be* casual, one can be accused of having a "studied casual manner." The writer INSINUATES that the newscaster is not really what he is trying to convince his audience he is. Hence the loaded term "studied" denigrates the newscaster. Notice, though, that there is nothing about the word *studied* in itself that is necessarily denigrating. The word becomes negative when it is used in conjunction with "casual." The same group of people could be called freedom fighters, guerrillas, raiding parties, goons, thugs, terrorists, or death squads, depending on the extent of the writer's sympathy with the group's politics. Or, in a variation on a famous example, consider "I am firm, you are stubborn, he is obstinate, but they are pig-headed dog-in-the-manger obstructionists." See CHARACTERIZATION, EVALUATIVE.

LOCUTION

A locution is a particular combination of words or a word taken to be characteristic of an individual or a group. Consider:

> "Did you finish that job?"
> "Damn straight, man."
> "I'm sorry, I'm not familiar with that locution. Does it mean something like 'I certainly did'?"
> "Yeah, right, and you want to know where you can put your 'locution'?"

LOGIC

Logic is the systematic study of the principles by which conclusions are drawn from a formulation of observations or ASSERTIONS. *A* logic is a particular set of such principles. To call the relations among a set of statements leading to a conclusion "logical" thus is to say that the principles of that particular logic have been followed. See DEDUCTIVE ARGUMENT and INDUCTIVE ARGUMENT. Also see EMOTION.

LOGIC, ARGUMENT FROM

Perhaps the strongest and most frequently invoked of what I refer to as authorizing tropes is that in which the writer asserts that the position she is opposing is "not logical" or says of her own position that it is "only logical." The writer is seldom referring to the actual drawing of inferences but rather to the doubtfulness or strength of the PREMISES. It is assumed, in other words, that that which is logical is either true or (at least) closer to the truth than that which is illogical. The employer of this trope takes logic to be a name for a process by which one arrives at truth, and so to designate something as logical is to privilege it, especially in relation to the illogical. The relation between logic and truth, however, is more complex (see VALID).

The writer employing logic as an authorizing trope assumes, as in the similar use of science (see SCIENCE, ARGUMENT FROM), that logic is not only monolithic (that is to say that it is only *one* thing), but that it has content, assumes in other words that one can "logically" determine if the premises from which one reasons are true. There are, however, many "logics" and many ways to reason. See TROPES, REASON, and especially EMOTION. See also *PATHOS* for the relationship of the trope to the triad of Aristotelian rhetorical appeals.

LOGOS

Logos is the third of the three modes of appeal in classical rhetoric (the other two being *ETHOS* and *PATHOS*). From a contemporary perspective *Logos* (usually capitalized) is a kind of catch-all word for all the concepts involved in an "essentialist" view of the cosmos. It means, variously, "Reason," "The Word (which is both with and of God)," and the "source of all Truth" (among a number of other things that a good dictionary will list). Please note the capital letters in the foregoing. Rather than to adopt the contemporary version of its use by rhetoricians (as opposed to rhetors) as involved in the speaker's attempt to gain the confidence of her audience (which I approach under the head of *ethos*), I have chosen to view it as part of the relativism debate. See TRUTH, REASON, and ABSOLUTE.

MAJORITY

An appeal to the majority is related to *AD POPULUM* and is often called "bandwagon." It is a characteristically

"American" and democratic appeal (being related to the notion of "majority rule"). According to this logic that movie is the best that does the greatest box office, the best books are the bestsellers, and if most people drive General Motors products, no more needs be said. Hence the irony of Thoreau's statement that he constituted a "majority of one." Thoreau, in this statement, invoked (and was one of the creators of) the American reverence for the individual that often operates in conflict with the democratizing aspect.

MEDITATION
The "meditation" is a written form of a mental practice, usually seen as religious, formally designated as *having no goal* and is in this to be distinguished from "contemplation," "deliberation," "consideration," or so-called "brainstorming," all of which are directed toward the solution of some problem. The importance of the meditation to rhetorical analysis is that the form, in its presumed lack of persuasive intent, carries the implication of sincerity. The writer with persuasive intent can thus utilize the form in her attempt to persuade, and, as is the case with any other deliberate use of language, the "meditation" becomes a construction intended to convey the *impression* of SINCERITY. See PERSUASIVE WRITING, INDIRECT ARGUMENT.

METAPHOR
Metaphor is closely related to ANALOGY but is usually treated as a clarifying device rather than as a type of argument. However, extended or not, metaphor functions as argument. Essentially a metaphor is a comparison of two unlike things intended to point up certain similarities between them. As such it is additionally related to ASSOCIATION in the ways it can function. An extended metaphor

may persist throughout a paragraph or even an entire essay, surfacing directly or indirectly at one or more points. Metaphors may be implicit or explicit, and one should be alert for the implicit. An example of this occurs in the statement under FACT, "They [facts] must first be put inside some theory." "Inside" here is the implicit metaphor. Involved is the notion that a theory can be metaphorically understood as some kind of a container. Students, after having Orwell presented to them, will sometimes decide that metaphor is a constituent of bad writing (that somehow the use of metaphor is an evasion of saying what something "really" is [see MEANING]). Our language, however, is constructed (!) on a foundation (!) of metaphor so deep (!) that we have forgotten the metaphoric implications of most of it. In what sense, for instance, do I "*go*" to sleep? How, exactly, does one "*pay*" attention? Consider the metaphoric implications of "see" as it is used in this glossary, that is, "see" (consult, refer to, look at, check) the glossary on (concerning, in relation to, about, in reference to) this. Consider also, in relation to my emphasis on the rhetoric of written argument, my continual use of "says" in reference to a written statement. See FIGURE OF SPEECH.

We easily recognize metaphors of the one-on-one type of, say, "The right to vote is the very *backbone* of democracy" but often do not *see* the ones that are *concealed* in the form of a verb. Nietzsche goes so far as to assert that metaphors are the way in which we know, and insofar as a metaphor is never the thing the metaphor refers to (as the name of a thing is not the thing), we are always at a metaphoric distance from reality, a distance that, due to the nature of language itself, we can never diminish.

Metaphors frequently carry within themselves limits imposed on conceptual attitudes toward areas of inquiry.

After an interviewee left the committee room, a senior colleague of mine (I was a very green first-year assistant professor at the time) commented that the candidate for a position in Victorian literature was very much on top of his subject. Would that I had had the sense not to speak my thought, but I exclaimed, "That's really interesting. I would have said that he was really into his subject." The silence that followed was deafening.

I don't think the sexual implications of the metaphor caused the awkward silence because the original metaphor ("on top of") carried sexual implications as well. Instead, I think that what I *had* signaled was a lack of respect for an attitude toward mastery of a subject expressed in terms of control. I became, with that statement, Ph.D. or not, "one of those hippies." I had suggested that areas of specialization are not capable of being "mastered," or "controlled," but instead that they can be "entered" and "explored," and perhaps I had suggested as well that anyone who claims control of an area of information is self-deceived. I had not *intended* such criticism of my colleagues, but it was implicit in the metaphor, whether I had it directly in mind or not.

Metaphors can and do involve attitudes, usually implicit, toward life-and-death issues with life-and-death consequences for those so represented. See, for instance, Orwell's assertion in the opening paragraph of "Politics and the English Language" that English-speaking cultures will survive or perish according to the metaphor they employ to express their attitude toward the language.

MIDDLE TERM
See DISTRIBUTION. The repeated term in a syllogism is the middle term.

MIXED METAPHOR

Unless she is trying to be funny, the writer who employs a mixed metaphor has forgotten that a given phrase *is* a metaphor. The person who writes that she would like "to orchestrate the landmarks in the history of her school" no longer understands that a "landmark" is a landmark precisely because it cannot be "arranged." Barney Frank provides some splendid examples and tops them up with a nice dollop of irony in a *Washington Post* article. Frank writes: "an anguished Republican insisted that the Democrats 'stop milking this dead horse.' (In a spirit of conciliation, one Democrat advised him in return 'not to carry all his spilt milk in one basket.'). But few metaphors can meet this standard." Many statements that have become clichés or are in the process of becoming clichés are metaphors. For a metaphor to function as more than a simple place marker or space filler, we need to be conscious of it as a comparison between discrete elements, and as a comparison we ask that it have more than one point of comparison, that, in other words, it be employed consistently. A metaphor is mixed when it breaks that consistency. Frank's examples are especially illustrative of this in that he breaks not just one metaphor, but two, and does so by combining them.

MODESTY

Lincoln's "The world will little note nor long remember what we say here, but it can never forget what they did here" may be the most famous American example of the AD POPULUM appeal to the virtue of modesty and its avoidance of the appearance of pride (which, we might remember "goeth before a fall" [see SAYING]) or arrogance. Although historically considered this constitutes an anachronism, a statement in which the writer denies her importance in the face of the importance of the subject of the argument might well be considered a staple of **ROGER-IAN ARGUMENT**. The writer is ostensibly searching for a solution to a problem rather than trying to "win" an argument. The person who responds to congratulations on some achievement by attributing her success to God or to the rest of the team or to a great teacher, or to her coach is also exercising this strategy.

One might wish to remember, however, that Winston Churchill, when told that the person who had defeated him for the position of prime minister was a very modest man, commented that the individual in question had a great deal to be modest about. See UNDERSTATEMENT.

MONOLOGUE

The essay, as a literary form, is characteristically monologic, that is, composed in one VOICE. A monologue is one person speaking without consideration of the direct reply possibility characteristic of DIALOGUE. The essay is, then, one person writing without consideration of direct reply. This single voice can, of course, incorporate dialogue as part or as apparent whole. The essayist thus can write an essay *as if* it were a dialogue. The so-called "Platonic Dialogues," for instance, are essays in which we must remember that Socrates and whoever else (Meno, Crito, Protagoras, etc.) are all aspects of the voice of Plato.

In one of its forms the essay can closely resemble the overtly dramatic form of the monologue, the soliloquy. Conventions governing the soliloquy dictate that the speaker is talking *to herself*, that is, that there is no consideration of the effect of the words on others and that it is hence utterly honest (see SINCERITY). The essay form that resembles this most closely is often called the "personal" essay and distinguished from argument. Historically it is akin to the meditation, in which, typically, the writer records herself thinking about religious subjects. The presumed honesty of the form is then reason for the persuasive essayist to incorporate aspects of the personal essay into the persuasive essay and reason for the content of the MEDITATION to be manipulated in whatever manner the writer would think most useful in accomplishing her persuasive end. See INDIRECT ARGUMENT.

MYSTIFY, MYSTIFICATION
As the word indicates, to "mystify" something is treat it as if it belonged in a special category of the difficult, obscure, or mysterious. If I say of something that it's a "mystery," I treat it as outside of the regular arena of argument and so privilege it as needing no defense. Theologically, a mystery is not understandable through reason but is nevertheless held to be true. If, however, I respond to some position with the statement "That's a mystification," I am claiming that it is not mysterious in nature but that the person doing the mystifying would like me to believe it is and so be spared the task of defending what may be an untenable attitude. Although to mystify and to complicate are frequently seen as related, their impulses are near opposites. See COMPLICATE.

NAME-CALLING
Name-calling is negative assertion. Barbara Lawrence, in an essay entitled "Four-Letter-Words Can Hurt You," writing about (not to) her students, says, "if they are *fans* of Norman Mailer [italics mine]. . . ." A "fan" is identified by blind, even "irrational," loyalty. Notice that she does not say "if they are *students* of Norman Mailer," or "if they are *aficionados* of Norman Mailer," or even "if they are *readers* of Norman Mailer." Lawrence's choice of "fan" denigrates

both Mailer's readers and Mailer himself (few who consider themselves feminists feel that Mailer deserved his Pulitzer Prize). Name-calling assigns someone or something to a category without offering any defense of that assignment. The device counts on the reader's assent to the categorization as fitting once it is presented (and, as I hope the example makes clear, on the target audience sharing the writer's attitude toward the term employed–in this case that being a "fan" is characteristic of a lower form of life than the intellectual). Name-calling is associated with AD HOMINEM and at an extreme with INVECTIVE. In its most subtle forms, name-calling is associated with LOADED DICTION.

NAMING

"Sticks and stones may break my bones, but names will never hurt me" might suffice to get one through some playground difficulties, but it is nonsense rhetorically. As with DEFINITION, it is difficult to overemphasize the rhetorical importance of naming. Consider, for instance, the names of the political action groups whose self-ascribed names have become the conventional references for the groups "choice" and "right to life." Were the groups naming each other, we might see something like "abortion on demand" or "freedom to kill" and "women as wombs." Or consider, in this light, the differences among the terms *contraceptive, contragestive,* and *abortifacient.* The group or person with an organization or a concept that needs a label for short reference will try to acquire a name that is distinctive and often, but not always, positive. Queer Nation, for instance, sought to APPROPRIATE a name given by the "straight" world to homosexuals as appropriate to its confrontational activism ("We're here, we're queer–get used to it"). It should be apparent that the range of social acceptability among the terms *gay, homosexual, invert, queer, fairy,* and *faggot* would make a good deal of difference in the lives of the people so classified. Muhammad Ali (a name change from what he called his slave name–Cassius Clay) defended his refusal to be inducted into the U.S. army to fight in Vietnam on the basis that "No Viet Cong ever called me nigger." People kill and are killed over names and, from their perspective, with good reason. The argument is that if you are named by another you are by that name classified and evaluated. If, for instance, women were legally forced to identify themselves as *Miss* or *Mrs.,* they would be subject to a system of classification that is not applicable to men (*Mr.* does not identify a man's marital status). Because no equivalent to *Mr.* existed for women, social pressure was applied to acknowledge the neologism *Ms.* (or, as I write it and as it is often written because it is a word itself rather than an abbreviation for one, *Ms*).

On the more overtly political front, think of the historical importance of naming those events that are referred to as "the Boston Tea Party," "Watergate," "Desert Storm," "Pearl Harbor," and "the Holocaust."

It is important to recognize that there is no name that can be considered the "real" name of anything (any more than one can say there is a real meaning for any given word) and that what entities are known as changes over time. The mechanism that decides what name will be used and how that name will be understood is social. Rhetoric, of course, is a key instrument in establishing that social status. See DEFINITION, TAUTOLOGY, and POLITICALLY CORRECT.

NARRATIVE, NARRATION
As an ANECDOTE is a brief story, a narrative is a longer story, the process of telling which we refer to as *narration.* We can also refer to the "narrative elements"

of a particular piece of writing. I can, for instance, present an argument in the form of a narration of those events and ideas I went through in arriving at the conclusion that I did.

It has been suggested numerous times that narratives are the most important of the linguistic behaviors we use to formulate what we think of as our "selves." "Tell me about yourself," for instance, invites the individual questioned to present "the" story of how she got to where she is when the question is asked. Putting events within the framework of a story gives us ways to arrange and then remember what becomes "significant" in that narration as we create what is important in the story of how we became whatever it is that we think we are.

Because narrative is so important to our idea of self, we tend to be open to other narratives in ways we may not be to particular positions. I can, for instance, hold members of the Ku Klux Klan in utter contempt, but nevertheless find interesting a clanswoman's narrative of how she came to the organization. Narrative frequently has an important place in argument, and some would suggest that all narrative, fictional or not, constitutes argument (and we must remember that we are all capable of remembering things "wrong" and of remembering things that never happened, in consequence of which the notion of maintaining a distinction between fact and fiction becomes problematic). The fiction becomes, in a sense, the facts that we select, from among the millions of events that constitute our pasts, as being important to our "story." See especially PERSON.

NATURE, ARGUMENT FROM
Like history, logic, and science, nature is referred to frequently in argument as if it were a single thing from which we can learn if we are able to read "it" correctly. I thus

classify the word as a metonymy and among the major authorizing tropes (see TROPE). To understand how much is justified in the name of nature, think about the privileging of that which can be associated with the "natural." We justify behavior, for instance, on the basis that it is "only natural." We think of nature as something that we can go out and be "in" and that doing so is good for us. Natural, at the moment, equates immediately with good, and the "artificial" and "synthetic" are sinister in comparison (despite nylon ripstop fabric being understood as great material for tents despite its lack of "natural" fibers). For the rhetorician it is interesting to note how nature is defined in the argument. Does it teach us "lessons" (like HISTORY)? Are volcanoes "just"? Are antibiotics "unnatural"? Answers to questions like these tell us a great deal about how the target audience is intended to privilege the term.

There are additional subcategories that are not only regarded as privileged but also, insofar as they are taken to be *aspects* of nature, assumed to be virtuous. Evolution, for instance, is one of these, and those who privilege nature see the process typically not only as good but also as "culminating" in *Homo sapiens,* an anthropocentric determination that argues for the tropic nature of nature so understood. There is no "reason," for instance (unless we similarly PRIVILEGE LOGIC), to think of *Homo sapiens* as a life form in any way superior to cockroaches (complexity and superiority seem to be negatively related here), and indeed, were our criterion for recognizing superiority the odds of survival, the cockroach wins "hands down."

NEOLOGISM   (NEE *ALL* UH JISM)
A neologism is a new word. New words are interesting to the rhetorician from a number of perspectives, but especially in relation to EXISTENTIAL IMPORT. One of the theses

of Orwell's *1984* is that control of the language is control of
what can be thought. Orwell's position is that if we do not
have a word for a concept, we cannot have the concept. In
"The Principles of Newspeak" he writes that the result of
adopting Newspeak and suppressing Oldspeak would be
that "heretical" thought "should be literally unthinkable, at
least so far as thought is dependent on words." A neologism, the reverse of this, is almost always in some way
heretical in that it represents the birth of a new thought, a
new concept or way of viewing the world. The notion of
"virtual reality," for instance, is neologistic, and we could
probably say it has acquired EXISTENTIAL IMPORT and is
"virtually" assured a place in the dictionaries of the future.
What remains to be seen is what effect the concept will
have on the idea of "reality" itself.

NON SEQUITUR   (NON *SEH* QUI TER)

Latin for "it does not follow," this term is so broad as to be
virtually useless to the analyst. It is the Latin equivalent to
replying to a claim that X is Y by saying "No, it's not."

NULL SET

In set theory the "null set" is the hypothetical set that has
no members. As with the set of all sets, which must, to be
the set of all sets, be a member of itself, certain conceptual
difficulties arise. The concept of "nothing" is in itself problematic. Can one, for instance, have a sense of "nothingness," and if one does so, does the nothingness then
constitute something? In what sense can nothing "be"? Is it
not nonsense to say that nothing "exists"? Fortunately the
human mind seems to be so composed that it can function
regardless of these conceptual knots and paradoxes. What
the rhetor needs to consider is if the argument under
analysis introduces null categories (no one, nothing,

nowhere) and from them claims to demonstrate the presence of some other thing. If such a claim is made it constitutes an ARGUMENT FROM IGNORANCE.

OBJECTIFY

A simple way to consider how this word is being used is to distinguish "object" from "subject." The subject "acts," the object is "acted upon." In its simplest meaning, to "objectify" means to render a group or member of a group as object rather than subject. Thus "I hug trees" is to "objectify" trees.

To "objectify," however, is intended to imply that so placing a group or member of a group is to reduce a complex being to an "object," when, from the perspective of the person using the term, the being should not be so considered. The word derives largely from feminist theory and is intended to describe, say, the process that allows a concept like a "trophy" wife or the description of people (not necessarily women) in terms of a portion of their anatomy. The "whole" person, as it were, is reduced to or thought of primarily in terms of that anatomical feature. When used in this sense, the word is not related to "objectivity." Presumably by "objectifying" people one seeks to gain power over them by avoiding the necessity of considering them as other than a "thing." The person, by the same token, who permits the "objectification" of herself participates in this degradation. Consider: X "shows the way women could be, not objects but subjects, not the other, but the self."

From the perspective of rhetoric, the whole process of naming a complex whole and considering it as a unity (the University of Houston, for example) participates in this process. The rhetorical analyst should question what complexities the process of NAMING involved here obscures and for what purpose the simplification is being used. At the moment, for instance, tobacco companies are spending a great deal of money on advertising devoted to associating raising taxes on cigarettes with "big government" abusing "working people." "Working people" are intended to resent being thus "objectified" and threaten to vote their representatives out of office unless the situation is remedied.

OBJECTIVE

An "objective" report is usually understood as one that lacks an *obvious* "subjective" bias. The "objective" reporter supposedly gives us "the facts" and refrains from "editorializing." A look at the entry for FACT should indicate some of the problems involved with this view. An honest reply to the request "Just tell me what happened" would have to be, "I can't. I can tell you only what I remember of what I saw from the position I occupied relative to the event. If I am being asked to report what I saw and omit what I felt, I must again reply that I can't, because what I saw (when I blinked, when I looked up or down, right or left) was influenced by what I felt to an extent that I can only guess at." Hence *all* reports are subjective, some obviously so, and some not so obviously so. Any attempt, then, to dismiss an argument on the basis that it is "only a subjective view" is wrong-headed. *All* arguments are subjective–and some are explicitly so. The modern rhetorician would use the word *objective* only to describe TONE, recognizing that an "objective tone" is a strategy used to influence a particular audience's judgment concerning the *ETHOS* of the writer. Thus to complain that a report "lacks objectivity" means, from the perspective of rhetoric, that the writer's tone is assumed to be inappropriate to the type of writing she is supposedly producing.

The reader should be aware, nevertheless, that there is a vocabulary that supposedly delineates points on a range between objective (positive) at one end and subjective (negative) at the other. Think of each of these words as it might be used to refer to testimony given in a courtroom.

    objective
    impartial
    disinterested
    uninterested
    subjective
    prejudiced
    slanted
    biased

Current conversational use of the word *take,* as in "What's your take on the Iraq thing?," offers an interesting commentary on the devaluing of the concept of objectivity. It seems to be a more metaphorically specific revision of the earlier use of *view,* as in, for instance, "What is your view of the current situation in Iraq?" The word *view* entails "a" rather than "the," recognizing that any view must be from a point and is therefore limited. *Take,* supposedly from film argot (as in "scene 1, *take* 24"), used in place of *view* adds a time dimension to the location dimension of the latter, underscoring that any statement emerges not only from a particular place but also from a specific time. See SUBJECTIVE.

OCCAM'S RAZOR
Also called the Law of Parsimony, Occam's razor (sometimes spelled "Ockham's") is the principle that says that given two equally satisfactory explanations for any given phenomena, take the simplest. The rhetorical trick involved, of course, lies in the notion of what constitutes "equally satisfactory." The simplest explanation for all manner of atmospheric anomalies, from one perspective, is extraterrestrials. But is it "equally satisfactory"? That depends on your criteria for that quality.

OED, **THE**   (OH EE DEE)

The *OED* is the *Oxford English Dictionary.* See CONNOTA-
TION; ETYMOLOGY, ARGUMENT FROM; and DICTIONARY. Far
beyond an unabridged dictionary, the *OED* is based on
historical principles and indicates not only the path taken
by a given word as it became written English but also,
by citation from period texts, the contributing lexicogra-
pher's sources for her derivations of the meanings that the
word has held while it has been a part of the written language. Any serious lexicographic investigation will include
consultation of the *OED.* Nevertheless, it must be noted
that no dictionary, the *OED* included, can be considered
definitive. It is, however, the dictionary that contains the
largest amount of data on the words it contains.

OMNISCIENT

The word *omniscient* describes what narrative theory (see
NARRATION) calls "point of view." The writer who composes
a narrative containing what X "thought" as X was doing y,
and further tells you what it *means* that X was thinking b
while doing y, has assumed an "omniscient" point of view.
She speaks, in other words, as one who knows all, not only
thoughts but also motivations and the meaning of actions
in the cosmos. Note that in the following the totality is
speculation. It is presented, however, from an "omniscient"
point of view. "She spent most of her day waiting for the
phone to ring. She hoped it would be him. But because she
knew it wouldn't be, she became the essential element in
the destruction of the last hope for the nation."

The "limited omniscient," much more frequently used,
stops making claims to knowledge earlier. The preceding example can be converted to a limited omniscient point of
view by inserting a "perhaps" or a "what might have been"

after "became." The limited omniscient thus is a more subtle manner of arguing than the omniscient on the basis that the writer tries to deny her omniscience, tries to appear modest or tentative about her abilities, and, if she is successful in this, masks previous claims to knowledge she could not have that occur prior to the admission of speculation.

OPINION

The word *opinion* is most problematic rhetorically in a question like "Is that a fact, or is that *just* your opinion?" Given that we have a rhetorically sophisticated understanding of what constitutes a "fact" (see FACT), we recognize that a fact means nothing outside of some theory, which *theory* is inevitably subjective. Hence the question is naive about "facts." If, however, we then ignore the first part of the sentence and concentrate on the second, then there are two possible readings: emphasizing the "your" or emphasizing the "opinion." If the emphasis is on the former, then the question expresses a lack of confidence in the *ethos* of the questioned. One might then reply to it, "No, it is not just *my* opinion, it is the opinion of most recognized authorities in the field." If this is the intent, then the question is legitimate. If, however, the emphasis is on "opinion," then, again, it is naive. As all views are in the final analysis "subjective," so also all statements are in the final analysis "opinions." This is not, however, to say that all opinions are of equal value. Obviously an opinion that is considered, judicious, and informed is to be trusted before one that is none of these. The point here is that it is no objection to a statement to claim that it is *only* an opinion, nor is it to claim that it is an opinion and not a fact. The question should not be "Is that an opinion?" but rather "On what do you base your opinion?" Calling a person "opinionated" usually means that you disagree with most of the positions that person expresses. It can also mean that the person in question expresses opinions rather than maintaining a facade of neutrality. When the term is used in accord with rhetorical principles, it refers to an *undue* adherence to opinions that are insufficiently considered or informed.

In another use the word is intended to call specific attention to a statement having been derived from the particular (and therefore limited) experience of an individual or a definable group. An individual might write something like, "That, however, is only my opinion, and I would welcome the views of others who might have had similar experiences." The intention here is to avoid sounding overbearing or imposing and to indicate a becoming humility in the face of other knowledge (see MODESTY).

OVERHEARD ARGUMENT

The open letter, a communication directly addressed to an individual but published where it can be read by anyone, when it succeeds, often does so not because the individual addressed is convinced by the material presented, but rather because the individual addressed knows that the contents of the "letter" are now public. In a smaller theater of endeavor, the "copy to" notation at the top or bottom of an electronic or hard copy memorandum or letter can serve the same purpose. A further rhetorical strength of the open letter is that it is difficult to reply to. As with the PARADOX of PROTESTING TOO MUCH, an "open" response is often seen as tantamount to an admission that the original open letter was justified, whereas the lack of a reply allows the original to remain unchallenged and thus, seemingly, acknowledged. Silence, per tradition, implies assent.

OXYMORON   (OXEE *MORON*)

An oxymoron is a self-contradictory phrase, sometimes deliberately humorous, sometimes not. Examples: *jumbo shrimp, plastic silverware, black light, nonstop flight, creation science, live recordings, holy war, vacuum packed, green oranges, legalized murder, true story.* There are specific reasons for each of these constructions, and the rhetorical analyst should consider what these might be rather than dismiss them as meaningless. Consider, for instance, the wit and the depth of the insult involved in the statement "*X* wouldn't recognize subtlety if you hit her over the head with it."

PARADIGM

A paradigm is a model for whatever set is under consideration. Members of the set are then judged in comparison to it. The paradigm thus defines the set it is a model for. That person who proposes and can then succeed in establishing a proposal as paradigmatic is in a very powerful position in relation to establishing the characteristics of the set. Is Muhammad Ali the paradigmatic boxer, or is Mike Tyson? If one believes that Bill Clinton can no longer be the paradigmatic president, can Jimmy Carter? Ronald Reagan? Who is the paradigmatic philosopher? Is it Socrates? Could it be Nietzsche? What follows if Diana Spencer is established as the paradigm for glamorous femininity? Paradigms are almost constantly being proposed, and their acceptance would seem to have little to do with the characteristics we would defend in the abstract. They seem instead to relate to a psychological response to a cultivated, or crafted, persona (the "Lady Di," beloved of thousands, bears little relation to the biological Diana Spencer). The rhetorical analyst needs to be sensitive to the proposal of a paradigm and then to the characteristics of that paradigm that may not be emphasized.

Because paradigms seem to be a, if not the, major way we organize our valuing of and relation to the world around us, we should consider from a more philosophical perspective what it is that we would take for the model of the world. Are we to conceive of it on the model of a machine, a made thing with a purpose, or can we conceive of it as an organism, a "born" thing whose only function is to live according to its nature? Do we view "reality" as the Holy Grail that we continually seek and that remains out of our grasp, or can we view it as a product of the human imagination?

PARADOX

A paradox is related to an OXYMORON, but a paradox is a *seeming* contradiction. In contemporary decor, for instance, the concept that "less is more" can be considered paradoxical. Or consider that the *more* you deny something, the *less* likely you are to be believed.

PARAGRAPH

The paragraph is the basic organizational unit of prose (poetry is sliced thinner in that the basic unit is the line, followed by the stanza). One is typically told that the paragraph represents one complete thought and that a paragraph division indicates the introduction of a new thought.

A little bit of thought, however, and observation of printed prose material indicates that this is a writing teacher's rule, not a writer's rule.

However, we can say that the length of the paragraphs in a given piece of writing offers a sort of index to the reading habits of the intended readers.

Take newspapers, for instance. There we typically find very short paragraphs, many no longer than a single sentence. Some no longer than a single word.

Really.

Writing, on the other hand, that is intended for a reader with a longer attention span, or with more time to appreciate the nuance and play of words and sentence structure in relation to the complexity of the ideas expressed, composed, formulated, tends not only to contain longer sentences but also to be composed of longer paragraphs, some so long, indeed, that one of them can be as long as the entirety of the journalistic production designed to be consumed in bits and pieces by consumers seeking information rather than edification. So, to some extent the length of the paragraphs in a given piece of writing is determined by the pacing the writer seeks. Short punchy sentences in short paragraphs encourage the reader to move quickly, whereas long sentences in long paragraphs encourage the reader to linger in consideration of the material being presented. Neither of these can be called more effective than the other, nor can one be considered to be more correct than the other. As always, the task of the analyst is to deal with what is presented in an attempt to determine by what means, through what resources of the language, the writer is trying to persuade her targeted audience.

PARASIOPESIS   (PARA SEE *OPE* UH SIS)

To use parasiopesis is to emphasize a point by passing over it, by mentioning specifically that you are *not* going to consider it. This is a device that political columnists are very fond of and that the Starr/Clinton wars have provided a particularly juicy occasion to exercise. For instance, "Let us leave aside that there have been *four* accusers (to date), and the questions raised in the Whitewater affair. Let us not mention the Asian connection, nor will we raise File-gate, or Travelgate, or even, for that matter, inhaling. Let us instead concentrate on what constitutes the *legal* definition of 'outrage.'" In her presentation of the list of what she is *not* going to mention, the writer does her best to put them immediately in front of the reader.

PARODY

A parody is an imitation of something that comments on what is being "parodied" in a usually negative way through exaggeration of what is presented as characteristic of the object. As is argued concerning satire, a case can be made that many subjects are parody-proof insofar as they cannot be exaggerated further than their normal mode (professional wrestling or drag-racing advertising, for example, or the deliberately ritualized such as graduation ceremonies, investitures, or the celebration of a High Mass).

An imitation is typically differentiated from a parody in that an imitation is valued for the accuracy of its representation rather than its ridicule of the subject imitated.

PASSIVE VOICE

Although passive voice is often held up as "weak" writing, skilled writers use it deliberately to emphasize the event in question rather than the origin of the event. To write "Congress passed X legislation yesterday" is not therefore "stronger" than "X became law yesterday"; it is rather a change in the *emphasis,* or at least an attempt to avoid involving the argument in a side issue (in this case the quality, or virtue, or the lack of it, of Congress). The writer is interested in discussing the *effects* of the law, not the wisdom of Congress.

PATHOS

In classical rhetoric, *Pathos* is one of the three basic appeals delineated by Aristotle as the means by which orators persuade. *Pathos* is, to vastly oversimplify, the appeal to emotion, which Aristotle differentiates from *Logos,* the appeal to logic, or reason, and *Ethos,* the appeal to character, the orator's presentation of herself to an audience as trustworthy and therefore believable.

PEOPLE, ARGUMENT FROM THE

This might also be called argument from *demos,* from the Greek word for the common people, from which we get our word *democracy* (not to mention *epidemic* and *demagogue*). Sometimes it involves the AD BACULUM—take the statement "The American people have had about enough of Kenneth Starr [the special prosecutor in the Clinton scandals]," which implies that if his activities are not terminated many members of the party with which he is associated will not be reelected—and sometimes it implies that wisdom lies with the most widely held opinion.

For the rhetorical analyst the problem becomes how the population referred to is defined and how its opinion has been sampled (if, say, fewer than five percent of eligible voters actually vote). The *demos* is referred to in many ways, among which are:

> the people
> people
> the man in the street
> the average American
> ordinary Americans
> the American people
> the public
> the populace
> the country
> my fellow Americans

If a speaker can give that group of people referred to a face, or defining characteristics, she has gained a powerful rhetorical tool in that when that population is invoked she can count on those characteristics accompanying the consideration. What are the implications, for instance, of Bill Clinton's reference to "Joe Six Pack"?

PERIODIC SENTENCE
When it is carefully constructed, and when that construction is not so complex as to make the structure hard to follow or lead the reader to ask how long this will go on before it gets to the point, the periodic sentence can be a graceful manner of emphasizing a point. The foregoing sentence is periodic in that it delays presenting its main clause until the end.

PERSON
In addition to being an available substitution for the word *man*, to bring sexist terms such as *chairman, spokesman,* and *salesman* into postfeminist discourse, the word *person* combined with *first, second,* or *third* refers respectively to these pronouns: *I* and *we* (and, I would argue, the more or less elegant and ambiguous *one*); *you* and *you* plural (and, if you are in the South, *you all*); and *he, she, it,* and *they.* "Proper" grammar would hold that the first, second, and third persons identify speaker, spoken to, and spoken about, but the language does not behave that precisely. The selection of person by a writer, like the selection of active or passive voice, is a stylistic choice based on the sought-after writer-reader relationship. Compare, for instance:

> "How is one to respond when one has been insulted?"
> "How am I to respond when I have been insulted?"
> "How are we to respond when we have been insulted?"
> "How are you to respond when you have been insulted?"

or

> "When someone insults one, what is one to do?"
> "When someone insults me, what am I going to do?"
> "When someone insults us, what are we going to do?"
> "When someone insults you, what are you going to do?"

I would suggest that in each case the movement from *one* to *you* simultaneously makes the question more immediate (less abstract) and emphasizes the commonality of the writer and the reader. This would be less emphatic were the writer or the reader British in that the use of *one* is frequently viewed by Americans as a Britishism, or simply as affected.

When a writer uses NARRATION, we enter another descriptive mode. The first-person narrator tells the story from her perspective: "I was run over by the truth yesterday, on my way to the gas station." The second-person narrator, like the third-person narrator, tells a story about the person addressed (that person may or may not be the person addressed in fact [see OPEN LETTER]): "Your twelve-year-old son is not home yet. You hope he is not with that kid down the street with the tattoo." The third-person narrator talks *about* someone, real or not: "She was waiting for the telephone to ring, hoping it would be an offer of immunity." Each of these allows the writer to work with the anecdotal (see ANECDOTE) with near complete freedom and to shape the narrative precisely to the demographics of the TARGETED AUDIENCE.

PERSONA   (PER *SEW* NUH)

Persona is related to but not identical with *ETHOS*. A male writer might, for instance, adopt the "persona" of a female in a particular piece of writing. The "persona" thus is whatever "character" or "role" the writer chooses to adopt for a particular piece of writing. Typically, however, the persona is *not to be identified with the writer in her own person.* However, the writer using a persona may not assume that the audience recognizes that a persona is being employed. A woman, for instance, writing in the persona of a man may not wish to encounter the response of an audience who knows that the writer is "really" a woman. The whole idea of a writer playing a role is rhetorically interesting in that it brings into question precisely what might be meant by that "really." Cary Grant, the actor, is reputed to have replied to an admirer who said that he had always wanted to be Cary Grant, "So have I." Grant means, presumably, that the person who is Cary Grant (born Archibald Alexander Leach) would like to have the qualities associated with the roles he has played. The rhetorical analyst should consider whether the writer wishes her persona to be recognized as such and what effect is sought.

PERSONAL ESSAY
See MEDITATION, SINCERITY, and PERSUASIVE WRITING.

The personal essay is traditionally distinguished from the persuasive essay–the former being devoted to creating "self-expression," the latter to convincing an audience on some particular subject. The personal essay, in that it proceeds from an exercise in "self-discovery," presumes that something has been discovered that is valuable and of potential value to others. The writer thus is presumed to have no designs on the audience but rather to want to share something with it from the most altruistic of motives. From a rhetorical perspective the personal essay constitutes an extended ANECDOTE, which the writer presents as in some way beneficial to the reader. From the perspective of the rhetor, *all* writing has a persuasive end, some of which is overt in its approach to that end.

Writing a personal essay may be an exercise in self-discovery or a form of meditation. Publishing such an essay, or submitting it to the attention of others, however, immediately brings it under rhetorical consideration.

PERSONIFICATION

To "personify" is to give human characteristics to that which is not human. One can refer to the thorns on a rose-bush as "vicious," for instance, or to hurricane winds as "furious." We frequently hear that Mother Nature has done something or other or even that love comes calling. This practice becomes rhetorically significant when the argument that so presents the object or concept then calls for us to respond to it as if it were human—to, say, reason with it, or discipline it, or forgive it. The nineteenth-century British cultural critic John Ruskin first challenged this practice, labeling it "the pathetic fallacy" and presenting the argument that such thinking interferes with a true appreciation of the world around. The sea, he pointed out, is neither cruel nor does it crawl, and to think of it in such terms can blind us to its beauty. We are also familiar with the concept of anthropomorphizing, as when we think of our computer as "stubborn" or our automobile as "sick."

Although our tendency to do this is often presented as a joke and merely made light of, it has extremely serious consequences in terms, for instance, of environmental issues, how we deal with predators, and so forth. It makes a great deal of difference whether we think of the world around in terms of Mother Nature or in terms of an ecosystem.

The rhetorical analyst should be alert for such usage and what is being urged on the basis of it. What is finally involved is as important as the whole of the authorizing trope, the ARGUMENT FROM NATURE.

PERSUADE

To persuade is to succeed in convincing. However, in rhetoric we label an essay "persuasive" if its *intent* is to convince, regardless of whether we judge it to be "successful" in this effort or not. What the rhetorical analyst needs to be attentive to is avoiding thinking that a writer persuades her audience by means of a particular device rather than considering that the writer *attempts* to persuade her audience by means of that device. See EFFECTIVE.

PERSUASIVE WRITING

It is pedagogically traditional to separate prose writing (writing that, unlike poetry must, with the exception of paragraph breaks, fill the area between the margins of the page or, in the quickest and easiest definition I know, that can be told from poetry because the latter crowds the middle of the page) into two major divisions, fiction and nonfiction, and the latter category into three major divisions: the PERSONAL ESSAY, EXPOSITION, and ARGUMENT. From a rhetorical perspective all these forms may be seen as having a persuasive intent. They differ in the relationship sought between the writer and the TARGET AUDIENCE. Consider the following list of prose types (bearing in mind that they can be mixed in any way the writer sees fit) as a series of groups constituting, in toto, a range of relationships from the (apparent) service provider of the expository end to "tables of testimony" (commandments) written with the finger of Yahweh on Mount Sinai.

exposition:
  instruction manual
  news story (reportage)
  report
  article
  notice
  note
  announcement
  report

exposition (privileged):
  meditation
  monologue(interior)
  essay (personal)
  letter

argument:
  editorial
  analysis
  review
  lecture
  homily
  announcement
  order
  directive
  command

argument (appropriated):
  consideration
  discussion
  dialogue
  deliberation
  debate

The reader is here cautioned that the following discussion of these more or less standard divisions of nonfiction prose is presented from the perspective of the analyst of rhetoric, that person who regards *all* written communication (including the note on the refrigerator door) as guided by a communicative/persuasive purpose. Thus the first of the four groups, here labeled "exposition," is, from the perspective of rhetorical analysis, that type of prose writing that *attempts* to create, in its target audience, the attitude that the writer is "objectively" presenting the FACTS relevant to a given subject. Exposition, from this perspective, is not a division of prose discourse according to approach, but rather represents a tone that the writer wishes the reader to accept as "factual." The writer of "exposition" cultivates a tone designed to allow (encourage) the reader to think that the writer has no specific interest in, or position in regard to, the subject matter presented.

The second group is made of those subtypes of prose currently called "personal," the first three constituting a division, along with prose fiction and poetry, of the curriculum of a good number of "creative" writing programs (usually called "the personal essay"). In rhetorical terms the form is a device designed to lead the reader to relax her critical/judgmental sense in the presence of the literary representation of a thoughtful person thinking deeply for no purpose other than to gain "understanding." The writer of the so-called "personal" essay *must* be SINCERE and thus without any designs on influencing the reader.

The third group, argument, splits into two groups: the first seeks the targeted audience's agreement, and the second demands it. Demands and commands, it should be clear, do not automatically elicit compliance, even if one is Yahweh. Both contain a combined argument from authority and argument from force (for instance, "'Shut up,' he explained").

The fourth group is referred to as argument "appropriated" in that, as a rhetorical form, it APPROPRIATES the forms of the forum, of the debate, the courtroom argument, the committee discussion, and so forth. In its written form it *is* none of these. Rather it attempts to look like and to sound like a representation of a contest in which the conclusion is *not* determined at the outset. The *writing*, however, coming after the real event it *may* be representing (it has no obligation to represent a "real" event—it can manufacture dialogue of the "would have said" type at will), will select and, unless it is merely a transcript, *must* select. This is to say that the rhetorical device involved is that it tries to *look like* the presentation of a transcript while presenting only that material the writer deems most beneficial to her position.

When I discussed this categorization—and particularly the idea that all nonfiction prose, including the note one writes to oneself and sticks on the refrigerator, is finally classifiable as argument—with my cross-town colleague, Alan Ainsworth, he suggested that the basic division with which I had begun—exposition, the personal essay, and argument—might be metaphorically understandable (because I had presented the range as from the writing of the note to the refrigerator to the inscribing of the Ten Commandments) in terms of thinking about expository writing as Adamic (naming and classifying), the personal essay as Satanic (rejection of authority in order to explore within the personal), and argument as the Yahwistic (instructing the chosen people who make up the "target audience"). The reader may find the metaphor helpful in that it is simultaneously clear in terms of the categories and inclusive, putting all three within a single organizing system. I wish to note, as well, as a reader pointed out, that the classification system is "very male." It may thus be very sexist as well.

PLATITUDE
See FOLK SAYING. A platitude may be considered as a folk saying that has become trite. In another view, all folk sayings are trite, and thus all may be considered platitudes. The rhetorician should consider what audience is being addressed with a statement like "You can't be too careful."

PLAY ON WORDS
Nat Hentoff, tireless defender of the First Amendment, writes of a ceremony at a Unitarian church where slips of paper upon which had been copied "patriarchal" excerpts from ancient and modern writers and philosophers were burned in a "pot" in front of the altar. A few paragraphs

later he refers to this as a "stirring ceremony." Given that the slips were burned in a "pot," and that slips of paper tend not to burn very well, and that Hentoff feels that the lesson learned from the ceremony by the children of the participants was "that the way to handle ideas they don't like is to set them on fire," the "stirring" ceremony which excited the participants is undercut for Hentoff's reader by the suggestion of the "stirring" that one normally does in a pot and how we use the term when we speak of "stirring up" trouble. Had the slips of paper been burned in a "crucible," Hentoff would not have been able to make the play on "stirring" that he does, but the reporter named a "pot," and Hentoff was able to make a subtle joke ridiculing the entire ceremony. Plays on words run the gamut from this level of subtlety to the heavy-handedness of the most appalling PUNS, typically counting on the reader recognizing that a given word is used in more than one sense. On the basis of the report that women find intelligent and informed verbal response the most attractive feature about a man, it was asserted that the more a man reads, the better he looks. The play is on the word *look*, which, as we know, can mean more than visual appearance. See EQUIVOCATION.

Other plays on words count on reader anticipation, particularly if they involve CLICHÉS. One wit, for instance, referred to a group of sports fans remaining loyal to their local team "through thin and thin," playing on the variation from the expected "thick and thin."

POLITICAL

Labeling something as "political" is often like labeling something as "rhetorical." The intended referent is, by the identification, being treated as discredited. It makes sense to say, for instance, "My motives are altruistic, and not in the least political" or "Do we have to politicize everything?" If we wish to discredit, say, attacks on the "personal morality" of the president, we can refer to them as being "politically motivated" and hence not to be taken as genuine. As with the term *rhetoric*, the assumption built into the negative of the term is that something can be *other* than political, which is as much as to say that it is virtuous to do something with total disregard for the consequences. The analyst should remember that the term *political*, like the term *politic* of which it is a form, can be intended as high praise as well. That which is "politic" can be being described as prudent, expedient, carefully considered, and conciliatory.

POLITICALLY CORRECT

The term *politically correct* was invented as an ironic referent to the constellation of social attitudes attributed to liberals of the "worst" sort, the "knee-jerk" liberals, so-called presumably because they act reflexively, without thought, automatically. In its original form its use indicated that the user was more traditional, or conservative, than the attitude being referred to.

Interestingly, what has happened is that increasing numbers of people are using the term to describe what they take to be simply the right thing to do. Note that straight-up racist and sexist terminology is not what is referred to, by contrast, as "incorrect." Rather it is terminology that has previously been more or less standard but that has become objectionable as the persons referred to have gained political power or recognition. Most often the "incorrect" term makes a distinction or fails to make a distinction that those referred to believe is damaging to them as a group. The term *Asian*, for instance, is the "correct" term for people formerly referred to as "Orientals." The term *orient* refers to coming from the east or, more specifically, where the sun rises. To refer to peoples from Asia as Orientals implies they are from "the east," which is a *direction* and can be a *place* only if one decides to locate it in reference to another point that would define the point of origin. The term *Hispanic*, referring to persons who trace their origins to Spanish-speaking countries or cultures rather than to persons who are citizens of particular countries, is "correct," as is *Latino*, although the latter is less formal. The "incorrect" is to refer to such persons as "Mexicans" or "Puerto Ricans," unless they are citizens of Mexico or Puerto Rico. It is similarly "incorrect" to refer to a person of Asian origin, resident of, say, the Chinatown of New York or Houston or San Francisco, as "Chinese" unless that person is a citizen of China. One would not, for instance, refer to a white citizen of the United States as "English" or "French," or "European."

Although the city that appears on old maps (in English) as "Peking" is now Beijing, Nippon remains "Japan," even though that name is an English pronunciation distortion as well. España remains "Spain," Deutschland "Germany," and "Italia" Italy, and so forth. Which terms thus are or are not politically correct will change over time as various of the groups denominated by the particular terms in question succeed in calling attention to the problems involved with the "usual" terms.

Some terms to consider are *handicapped* rather than *crippled, women* rather than *girls* or *ladies, substance abuser* rather than (depending on the "substance" referred to) *junkie, dope addict,* or *drunk; gay* and/or *lesbian* rather than *queer* or *dyke,* and so forth. See NAMING.

POST HOC, ERGO PROPTER HOC (HOC OR HOKE; LATIN FOR "AFTER THIS, THEREFORE BECAUSE OF THIS"; OFTEN SIMPLY CALLED *POST HOC*)

This is an assertion that the *simple* precedence of one event is sufficient grounds to assume a causal relationship to an event following. The implied weakness is always that the assumption fails to take into account *other* possible causes. The so-called "post hoc" fallacy is frequently invoked as a refutation of a given argument. Bear in mind, however, that although it does not follow that because one event occurs after another that the first caused the second, it does not *therefore* follow that it did *not*. Our current understanding of physics is that a "cause" *precedes* an effect.

POSTMODERN

With this term, as with several other "post" constructions, it is important to remember that *post* means "after," rather than "different from." Think, for instance, of the term *postwar*. It is to be contrasted with *prewar*, rather than *war*— that is to say it is taken to mean that after the war everything was different than it was before the war. The contrast is not thus between modern and postmodern, but rather between postmodern and premodern. Overall it is assumed that "modernism" was a postromantic position in which there was no accessible order or authority on which an organization of data could be based. The givens are, and are taken as inescapable rather than as an achievement, that all order and structure to be found are created by the mind itself. There are thus no "truths" or "eternal verities" to be appealed to for the resolution of argument. Because all truths are temporal, rather than eternal, one is "free" to do what one likes with the orders of the past. To put it another way, one can make up what one likes, taking whatever from the past one wants to. No tradition is PRIVILEGED, nor is a particular philosophical orientation. The term is frequently used in two differing ways: as a description of the way things are, and as a description of how irresponsible people wish to indulge themselves. This glossary is distinctly a postmodern document. See, for instance, the entry for TRUTH. My rhetorical choice of subtitle (A Contemporary Glossary) was fairly simple. I wished to avoid the negative reaction that many hold against the term *postmodern* (in which group I include myself, insofar as I think current thinking about "reality" should be called, instead, *postromantic*) but at the same time to convey the idea that the book is very much concerned with being in and of the world at this moment.

PREACHING TO THE CONVERTED

Properly speaking, preaching to the converted is not arguing. Generally the phrase is used to mean something like "wasting time" in that there is no apparent *point* in preaching to those who are *already* believers. If I say to someone, "You're preaching to the converted," I presumably mean "Stop trying to persuade me, I am already persuaded." But there are other reasons to preach to the converted, one of which is to reinforce a feeling of community or solidarity. This is the sort of "argument" that goes on at a political convention in which the "thesis" is the already agreed-upon "Republicans are good, Democrats are bad" (or vice versa). So, when one preaches to the converted, one's thesis is usually something that the target audience would take as a given, such as "Righteousness is good, sinning is bad." What one is trying to establish with such "argument" is a sense of solidarity and purpose that will inspire some particular action (picketing abortion clinics, for instance). The larger issue involved here has to do with EITHER/OR THINKING in relation to the question of audience, in general, and

TARGET AUDIENCE, in particular, and the relationships among overt, implied, and covert theses. See THESIS.

PREMISE

A premise is one of at least two propositions, or statements, or assertions, upon which an argument is based. Such a premise may be either stated or implied. The premises of a given argument are typically distinguished from the "conclusion," but that "conclusion" may then become a premise in a following argument. In the categorical syllogism (see SYLLOGISM), there are four acceptable forms for premises: "All A is B" (the "universal affirmative"), "Some A is B" (the "particular affirmative"), "No A is B" (the "universal negative"), and "Some A is not B" (the "particular negative"). Further forms are the HYPOTHETICAL, "If A, then B," and the DISJUNCTIVE, "Either A or B." See discussion of informal "either/or" forms at EITHER/OR and see ENTHYMEME.

PRESCRIPTIVE

A definition (as in this glossary or in a dictionary) can be placed within a range of views between the (now-discredited) notion that words have a "proper" or "correct" meaning and the view that words mean what they are used to mean in the community of those using them. The latter is the "descriptive" view, the former the "prescriptive." The emphasis in descriptive linguistic approaches is on understanding rather than "correcting." The 3,350-page *Webster's New International Dictionary of the English Language*, Second Edition, Unabridged, 1947, for instance, does not contain the word *shit*, presumably on the basis that it is not a "proper" word. The distinctly descriptive 8.9-megabyte *American Heritage English Dictionary*, Second Edition, 1.06, 1991, presents one intransitive and two transitive definitions of the word as a verb, eight as a noun, one as an interjection, one as a phrasal verb, five idioms, and an etymology of the word from Germanic through Old High German, Old Norse, and Old English. See RULES.

PRIVILEGE

To privilege an argument or a position is to grant it special status. The Constitution, for instance, is privileged in ways other laws are not in terms of the difficulty of amendment and repeal. The word *privilege* is often used negatively, especially by communities that consider themselves to be democratic. From one perspective, for instance, one could say that the basic idea behind "affirmative action" legislation is to privilege groups that had previously been the victims of negative discrimination. Another group could respond by saying that a particular group ought not be the recipient of "special" privileges, which would tacitly admit the charge. To privilege, in other words, is to treat as special, as different. The accusation that X or Y is being privileged can be either negatively or positively loaded, depending upon one's thesis (see LOADED DICTION).

PROBLEMATIC (NOUN)

As an adjective, *problematic* simply assigns the subject discussed *as* problematic to the category of problems without immediate and obvious answers. As a noun, however, the subject is assigned to *a* problematic, a specific arena of discussion belonging to *that* subject and to that subject only. Something that is simply problematic, such as the question of whether civil law should permit same-sex marriages, is capable of resolution at some point in the future. That which participates in the arena of *a* problematic, on the other hand, such as the question of how language can comment on itself, does not seem to admit of an answer but rather constitutes a problem of which the theorists and practitioners need to be aware.

PROLEPSIS

Prolepsis is the anticipation of and answering of an argument before it has been made. In writing it is less impressive than in a live situation, but it remains a powerful tool if it can be handled in such a way as to appear to be a fair representation of an opposing position.

PROOF

The Victorian playwright, essayist, epigramist, and wit Oscar Wilde wrote that "Even things that are true can be proved." That the statement makes any sense at all is a testament to the complexity of the meanings of the word *prove.* Technically, a proof is that which is accepted by a specific population (group) as sufficient demonstration of the consistency of a given statement with agreed-upon principles. Note here that what is accepted as established is the VALIDITY of an argument *within a given system of thinking.* Thus, for instance, in mathematics I can prove theorems until the cows come home without having made any statement whatever about their TRUTH. Outside of this technical definition, however, how are we to understand the term? Naive use makes "proof" of something tantamount to establishing its "truth," and that in an absolute (not relative) sense—that is to say, for now *and all time.* How might we go about "proving" (in these terms) the seemingly simple statement "All men are mortal"? The statement would be "proved" only when all men (people) were dead. Thus the last person alive could not verify the statement (even by dying) because she would not be around to register the proof. This is not an especially isolated case. It applies to *any* condition *still extant in the world.* We can say with a high degree of certainty that all dinosaurs were mortal, but to prove it we would involve ourselves in the argument from ignorance. We would have to argue that all dinosaurs were dead on the basis of not having any reports of living specimens for some time. Hence, in a reversal of Wilde's statement, we can say that even things that have been proved are not therefore true.

We must think of this as well in terms of the often-referred to "scientific proof." Scientists themselves, usually, are not guilty of claiming to have achieved "proof," but the public and the media are frequently to be found making statements like "science has shown us . . . ," or "it has recently been scientifically demonstrated that . . . ," or "the existence of black holes was proved last week by . . . ," and so forth. Scientific reporting of the same data would be more like "additional evidence supporting the X hypothesis was found last week by . . . ," and "a study of 525 white men, followed for fifteen years, indicates a much stronger than heretofore postulated link between A and B." Think back, for instance, on nutrition "theory" over the last four or five years for a perspective on "scientific" proof. The most common misuse of the term *prove* occurs when the writer intends to say that evidence supports, or additional evidence makes more likely, or that arguments have been advanced in favor of, and so forth. Remember that even in a court of law, the requirement is that the guilt of the accused must be "proved" "beyond a reasonable doubt." Brief consideration should make clear that one person or a group of people can hold that guilt has been proved beyond a reasonable doubt *when the accused is innocent.* To "prove," then, in at *least* this circumstance, is less than establishing as *true,* and thus less than absolute.

The rhetorical analyst should bear in mind as well that in popular usage the word *prove* is most frequently used as synonymous with "support."

PROPOSITION
A proposition is a statement upon which an argument is based. In formal logic a proposition is a PREMISE.

PROTESTING TOO MUCH
By long-standing tradition, silence implies assent. Thus not to reply to an accusation is often taken as an acknowledgment of the truth of the accusation. There is a story that Lyndon Johnson early on in his career as a politician suggested planting a rumor that his political opponent of the moment had had carnal knowledge of his hogs. When it was suggested that a problem with this was that it was not true, Johnson is said to have replied, "Of course it isn't, but let's make him deny it." The trap here is fairly clear. *Not* denying an accusation tacitly confirms it. Denying it calls attention to it. When to protest, and what to protest, thus often involves fairly delicate questions of judgment. Protesting "too much," however, involves not only making a denial but also repeating that denial with such vigor that it calls the denial itself into question. An example of this is the (former) TV evangelist Jim Bakker's denial of the statement by a former member of his staff that he had had homosexual relations with Bakker. Bakker replied that he had never had homosexual relations with anyone, and particularly not with this individual.

PUN
A pun is a play on words, usually in some very obvious, or even outrageous way, which is probably why it is sometimes called the lowest form of humor. It has been my

experience that poets, whom one might expect to find puns beneath their consideration, are often fond of them to the point of addiction. The poet Elder Olsen told me there is only one perfect triple pun in the language, "perfect" meaning that there is no dependence on mere similarity of pronunciation (as there would be if I asked, "Are we having pun yet?"). The phrase had to be spoken initially, but then could be spelled as "where the sons raise meat" or "where the sun's rays meet." From the poet's perspective, puns may represent a willingness to play with language and to exploit the relationship among homonyms created by the frequent friction in English between the way a word is spelled and the way it is pronounced as well as between the way words appear on the page and the way we understand them when spoken ("José, can you see," "Gladly the cross-eyed bear").

The extended form of the pun is the shaggy dog story, in which an extremely elaborate story is told for as long a time as the audience will bear and ends in a line that, it is hoped, will produce not laughter, but groans. Some of these are so well known that there are shaggy dog stories based on earlier shaggy dog stories that are simply alluded to in the punch line. See if you recognize any of these: "Where were you when the fit hit the shan?" "People who live in grass houses shouldn't stow thrones," "I wouldn't send a knight out on a dog like this," and "He was immediately arrested for transporting underage gulls across staid lions for immortal porpoises."

I have heard it suggested that a really good pun is the one that is met, not even with groans, but with dead silence, after which everyone gets up and leaves the room (part of the joke may be that real humor is no laughing matter).

Rhetorically, the hoped-for effect of the pun has to do with the *ethos* the writer would like to project—of a person who is clever, unpretentious, and able to view whatever subject is being treated with a sense of humor. This *ethos* can be particularly useful in a subject area where a good deal of the argument is being conducted in a somber and high moral tone. In such circumstances a joke, and especially one that is deliberately bad, can relieve a lot of negative tension.

PUNCTUATION

Although it may seem initially too obvious to require comment, there are a number of ways in which punctuation is employed to forward an argument and sometimes to create a VOICE. One of these, the use of quotation marks, is discussed in the entry for SO-CALLED. Another is discussed in the entry for ELLIPSIS. Italics can be used to highlight for the purpose of calling either negative or positive attention to a particular verbal construction, as can the exclamation point in parentheses or brackets (depending on whether it is inside or outside of a direct quote). The use of capital letters for words not normally capitalized can be a means of ridiculing something by rendering it as pretentious or self-important. It can also be used to indicate a quality of sound and intensity, as, say, in "after politely inquiring if there is some need to be satisfied, or if the furniture is perhaps less than comfortable, or the room temperature in need of adjustment, one is tempted to say, simply, 'SIT DOWN AND SHUT UP.'" Like emoticons and little smiling faces to dot "*i*'s" and question marks in a series (?????), many of these can be taken to indicate a simple and annoying "cuteness" or "bubbly" quality that is difficult to take seriously. As with the use of CLICHÉS, however, what is offensive to the analyst is a likely indication that the offended reader is not among the target audience for the piece so written.

Q.E.D. (CUE EE DEE)

Q.E.D. is an abbreviation for the Latin *quod erat demonstratum,* or "which was to be demonstrated." It should be read as the equivalent of "I rest my case. I have presented sufficient evidence to convince any reasonable person." See *ERGO.*

QUALIFICATION

As with WARRANT and CLAIM, one needs to know if argument is being discussed in Stephen Toulmin's terms or as the term is usually understood. In Toulminic terms, *qualification* is the specific limitation put on the claim (thesis) by the writer advancing the argument. For the rest of the world, a qualifier is a qualification, that is, not an observation of a limitation, but rather a clarification of the domain of the statement qualified. An example: "The conduct of education is too important a matter to be left in the hands of administrators and their sycophants who aspire to power and financial advancement. But I fear I will be misunderstood, so let me qualify that statement. An 'administrator' should be understood as precisely that—one who carries out the wishes of those who have employed him, or her, for that purpose. An administrator is *not* a CEO, is not an executive officer, although the 'professionalizing' of the academy has many so believing."

QUID PRO QUO

This Latin phrase translates something like "this for that," implying almost always an equal exchange. In argument it implies a fair settlement between two positions that agree, as it were, to lessen hostilities while continuing to disagree. See CONCESSION.

REASON

Since rhetoricians have begun to deal with ROGERIAN AR-
GUMENT and Toulmin's work with WARRANTS, and since
post-Nietzschean and post-Freudian thinking in general,
notions of what we might be talking about when we refer
to "reason," or "the reason," have become considerably
more sophisticated, more complex, and more problematic.
Man (*Homo sapiens*), we are told, is the "reasoning animal." She can sit down and "think things out," or "reason
things out." In this sense "reason" is the name of an apparent faculty that permits orderly consideration of alternatives in a problem situation. *Reasoning* thus is a deliberate
process of thinking used for problem solving. The process
of employing reason is referred to as being characteristic
of "rational" beings. To behave in a "rational" manner is to
behave according to the dictates of reason.

The rhetorician needs to be aware that in the West reason has historically been held to be humanity's Godlike
faculty, the cultivation of which not only ennobles humanity, but also leads it to the "truth" (see TRUE). Thus, presumably, all reason is part of *one* process, and that process,
if practiced appropriately, will, finally, lead all practitioners to the same solution. Alternative answers to a problem
can be comparatively evaluated on the basis of their "reasonableness" by logic–a systematic development of a set of
rules to determine the accuracy of a given process of
thought–the primary tool for the determination. Further,
emotion is seen as, at best, a source of *distraction* from reason, and at worst, as the destroyer of reason–its enemy and
antithesis. The admonition to "calm down," for instance, is
not far from the plea to "be reasonable." In Western soci-
eties reason has typically been held to be more abundant
in males and emotion more abundant in women (man
having been created in God's image, and woman from

man, and hence further from divine reason). The eighteenth-century Scots philosopher David Hume famously, and notoriously, argued that reason is and ought to be "passion's slave." His point was that "passion," or emotion, is prior to any process of reasoning–that it is passion that determines what it is that we reason about.

It is being argued with increasing frequency that to think of human problem solving solely on the basis of reason is naive and simplistic–instead, human beliefs and behaviors should be understood by considerations of the actual processes used in problem solving and knowledge acquisition (part of the field of study of these processes is called "cognitive science"). Arguments, it is argued, are not won or lost on the basis of reason, but rather on the basis of the satisfaction of certain psychic needs that they provide.

The rhetorician must pay constant attention to the degree to which the writer in question is defending her assertions by claiming their agreement with, or accord with, reason. To say that X is reasonable and Y is not (and is therefore "unreasonable") begs the question by means of loaded diction. As much as adherents of any particular system might like to think so, no idea's "reasonableness" is self-evident. See EMOTION, LOGIC, and particularly the subcategory under its own heading, DEDUCTIVE REASONING.

RECOLLECTION, DOCTRINE OF

This concept is extremely important to argument in general, but it is so seldom directly referred to that it is difficult to justify a glossary entry for it or even to know how to allow the reader access to the idea, which is much more prevalent than its name. The entry for *TABULA RASA* refers to the doctrine of recollection in that it was, in a number of ways, the concept in opposition to which John Locke formulated his "blank slate" metaphor.

Put simply, the doctrine argues that the truth is not deduced from our experience with the material world. Rather, our experience with the material world "reminds" us of what we already know but, in the trauma of birth, forgot. (Freud is here interestingly prefigured, in that the idea strikingly resembles his notion of the content of the unconscious mind that the therapist works to recover. A major difference, however, is that the repressed memory in Plato is of universal rather than particular and biographical truths.) We do not, in other words, "discover" the truth, as something that was out there for us to stumble over or not, but rather we "remember" it, a process that is more efficient with the help of a philosopher like Socrates, or a therapist, preferably Freudian.

As with the entry for *tabula rasa,* the rhetorical analyst is urged to consider the epistemological basis of the position under analysis. Those arguments that are finally reducible to principles that the arguer believes are "self-evident" (as opposed to "holds as self-evident") nearly inevitably invoke some version of the doctrine of recollection.

RED HERRING

To employ a "red herring" is to attempt to draw attention away from the main issue onto a side issue, to deliberately distract the speaker or audience from the course of the argument in order to avoid the conclusion that would, without the distraction, be drawn. By tradition, herring, a strong-smelling fish, was used by peasants, for whom wild game was a dietary essential, to draw the hunting dogs of the aristocracy off the trail (thus preserving for the peasants the game to be "poached," or illegally captured). Rhetorically the issue is whether the subject raised in the discussion *is* a red herring, or if it is a relevant issue.

REDUNDANCY

A writer who is redundant repeats herself. This repetition is sometimes deliberate. A few examples are "secular humanist," "past history," "inadvertently forgot," "very unique," "true facts," "new beginning," and, from the Weather Channel, "[Take a] look at Texas, still continuing to remain dry." In military systems redundancy is very often deliberate in that if one has *more* of a given item than seems immediately necessary, one can go on if one or several break. Aircraft carrier flight-deck crews apparently repeat their orders again and again to each other, constantly checking up. A copy of a piece of computer software is in one sense redundant, but in another sense simply insurance. Redundancy is more common in speech (where the speaker cannot count on the audience hearing or paying attention to every word) than in writing. Direct repetition, a form of redundancy, is often used for effect. Lincoln wrote, "we cannot dedicate–we cannot consecrate–we cannot hallow" in the "Gettysburg Address." He could have written "we cannot dedicate, consecrate, or hallow . . . ," and avoided the redundancy. It should be clear that redundancy is not necessarily a fault.

REFUTE

To refute an argument is to *succeed* in disproving it. It is not simply to argue against it. Part of the confusion involving the use of this term probably comes from the descriptive classical rhetorical name for that section of an argument devoted to attempting to disprove an argument–the "refutation." So also with "rebut." To rebut is to disprove, but in that courtroom use includes "rebuttal witnesses," and the concept of rebuttal as implying "reply," the word is frequently seen as a name for an *attempt* to

disprove with no necessary implication of success. See
SOCRATIC METHOD.

REIFY   (REE IH FIE)
To reify is to make, or treat as if, concrete, or material, an
abstraction. The clock, for instance, reifies the abstraction
"time." Dylan Thomas wrote that "time has ticked a heaven
round the stars," which can be read as saying that when
time becomes reified (clock-measured–"ticked") humans
become aware of death and of a "lifetime" as a measure of
a limit, thus leading to ideas of an afterlife (heaven) where
before there were only stars. Often the purpose of a
METAPHOR is to reify, to attempt to render an abstraction as
concrete. If I say that love is like a seesaw, I have attempted
to reify an abstraction. See EXISTENTIAL IMPORT, ABSTRACT,
and CONCRETE.

RELATIVE, RELATIVISM

> "I don't see how anyone can have children in this day and
>   age. It seems to me irresponsible."
> "I'm pregnant."
> "That's great."
> "Just seven seconds ago you said you were against having
>   children. That's totally inconsistent."
> "Well, that was seven seconds ago. A lot has happened
>   since then."

Here we have an instance of the relativity of "time" meas-
ured against intensity of moment (event). How long does it
take something to happen? That it was not so sixty seconds
ago does not indicate that it is not so now. So also if it was
seven seconds ago. If there is change it can happen
nowhere else but "in time," sometimes abruptly, sometimes so gradually that the change is not noticed.

That which is relative is that which is not ABSOLUTE. The principle of "relativism" is extremely important in contemporary argument. Consider, for instance, the idea of moral relativism, which holds that that which is immoral at one time may not be immoral at another time or that that which one particular group holds to be immoral holds no authority over a different view held by another group. Generally, from within a "relativistic" ethic, it is seen as appropriate to judge the morality of an act from within the standards of the group in question (see DOMAIN). Difficulty occurs when the actions of one group impinge on those of another, or when "group" membership is redefined so as to make an individual or a set of individuals a member of two groups simultaneously. If one is a Roman Catholic *and* a woman, for instance, one could see a conflict between equal gender rights and the pope's negative position on women as priests. What is important from the perspective of rhetorical analysis is the recognition of whether a given argument is being made from a relativistic or from an absolutist position, and when *that* determination has been made, to determine the source of the authority, in the case of absolutism, or the definition of the group, in the case of relativism. The foregoing brief discussion is a vast simplification of a hugely complex matter, the importance of which probably cannot be overstressed. Emerging questions of "rights" and obligations and social necessity hinge on the conflicts involved between and within these major conceptual differences.

There are a number of attacks on the concept of relativism, each of which makes sense from within an absolute system, so that each of which is without the domain of relativistic considerations from the start. The most frequently encountered response is that if "everything is relative" then it therefore follows that everything is equal–that it does not, in other words, in a relativistic system, matter what one does in that one thing is as good as another, indeed, as good as *any* other. What relativism says, however, is that all values exist within systems (see DOMAIN) and that how a thing is valued depends upon what system one judges it in. That is to say that the only attack on relativism that is mountable is that which asserts that it is not in accord with "real" values, which are universal (despite the fact that only a certain group of people thinks so).

More subtle is the approach, presumably describing relativism, that implies an absolute without asserting it. An example of this approach is the parable of the blind men and the elephant, in which one, at the tail, describes the elephant as very like a rope; one at a leg, as very like a tree; and the third at the trunk, as very like a vine. This parable is often given as an illustration of how it is that honest people can differ concerning a single subject. What is problematic about the parable from a relativistic point of view is that it presumes that were the men not *blind* they would *know* that the perspective of each of them was limited to what he could reach and that an elephant "really" is a combination of like a rope and a tree and a vine (plus some other stuff). That is, simply, that there is a perspective from which one can know the "reality," as it were, of an elephant. Thoroughgoing relativism, however, would say that the sighted person (who can see the totality that the blind [and, interestingly, unmoving] perceptors cannot) *still* does not see *the* elephant, which is finally knowable only as a construct of the perspective from which it is viewed. To put it as simply as possible, the relativist denies that anyone can answer the question "What is an elephant, *really?*" The relativist might answer, "That depends on whether one is an elephant, an animal trainer for a circus, a zoo keeper, a gardener, a taxidermist, an environmentalist, a biologist, or a Republican."

From here we encounter the assertion that because each of these views is, as it were, "partial," there must be a view that constitutes the totality of these views and that *that* view presents the real elephant. The being who could have such a view would, of course, have to be capable of being in all locations and all times (we have so far not discussed the problem of the "same thing" being different at different times–the elephant, for instance, at six months versus the elephant at sixty) simultaneously. As then is the case in the argument from design (see TELEOLOGY, ARGU-MENT FROM), one ends up inventing or assuming a divine figure to rescue an otherwise insupportable concept of objectivity, and with that divine figure, a "reality" that only those on especially good terms with that divine figure can access and then disseminate to the rest of us.

RHETORIC

Rhetoric has a multitude of definitions. The definition used here is "the use of written language to persuade." Rhetorical analysis, then, is analysis of the means a given writer uses in an attempt to persuade. Notice that the definition avoids BEGGING THE QUESTION in that using written language "to persuade" is different from "persuading by means of written language." For the rhetorician, I hope obviously, the pejorative phrase "that's just rhetoric" expresses a naive and limited definition of the term that restricts it to referring to the use of language to deliberately deceive and mislead. Although thirty-five percent of the use panel for the *American Heritage Dictionary* held the phrase "empty rhetoric" to be redundant, for the rhetorician it is rather the claim that a piece of writing is "only rhetoric" that is redundant. A written argument, from the rhetorician's viewpoint, cannot be *other* than rhetoric, so it *must* be "only rhetoric." A question that may clarify the issue is "If X argument is 'just rhetoric,' how could it be restated so that it was not 'just rhetoric'?" What would be removed from an argument to take the "rhetoric" out? Because from the perspective of the rhetorician all aspects of the arrangement of language toward the end of persuasion are rhetoric, the answer to the first question is that it could not be restated and remain the same argument, and if it were restated, not only would it be a different argument but also it would still be rhetoric. When the rhetoric is removed from an argument, there is *nothing* left–the rhetoric *is* the argument. What the person who complains that an argument is "only rhetoric" usually means is that although she disagrees with the conclusion being presented she cannot think of an immediate counterargument.

RHETORICAL ANALYSIS

Rhetorical analysis is near-allied to what linguists refer to as "discourse analysis" and related to what in psychology is referred to as "transactional analysis." In barest terms it is an attempt to account for the components of what is referred to as a persuasive essay in terms of how the writer intends for them to work to persuade members of the TARGET AUDIENCE of her THESIS. Specifically it treats each of these components as representing deliberate and conscious choices made by the writer in an attempt to achieve a desired persuasive goal.

As in any other analytic procedure, that analysis is deemed best that accounts for the largest number of data. For instance, in my discussion of the concept of a covert thesis (see THESIS), I briefly present a hypothesis to account for specific details of Gilbert Highet's rhetorical analysis of the "Gettysburg Address," which hypothesis, in my view, explains what Highet was trying to accomplish in terms of this covert subthesis. The reader is, of course, not obligated to accept this hypothesis, but if she does *not* she is, under the general notions of analysis, obliged to present a *more* satisfactory (more inclusive) explanation of these details. If this is done, a more satisfactory hypothesis is presented, specifically, an analysis that accounts for these *and* previously unaccounted-for data. There is no end to the process, nor is there a source of verification outside of the text itself (although, because all texts exist in specific places/times, there is no end either of supporting or corroborative contextual data that can be brought to the argument).

To repeat a central concern of the introduction to this glossary, the point of this process is that by becoming an active (as opposed to a defensive or even in the usual sense a "critical") reader one assimilates, accumulates, acquires a constantly wider range of options in accomplishing one's own rhetorical goals. Put again simply, the better one can read argument, the better one can write it.

RHETORICAL QUESTION

A rhetorical question is one the writer (or speaker) assumes will be answered in only one way and is hence not a "question" at all, but rather an invocation of a kind of choral response that she hopes will establish a bond between her and the audience. "The previous administration has given us higher taxes, fewer services, more waste, and more corruption than any administration in history. Do we want four more years of this?"

RIGHTS, ARGUMENT FROM

"We hold these truths to be self-evident, that all men are endowed by their Creator with certain inalienable rights, that among these are life, liberty, and the pursuit of happiness." Fill in the blank: "I have a right to _____."
Like the term *free*, as in "It's a free country," the term *right* can be used in reference to anything. We have "human

rights," "civil rights," the "right to privacy," and recently the tobacco companies tell us we have a "right" to smoke at the same time antitobacco lobbies tell us we have the right to be free of exposure to smoke. There are arguments concerning a "right" to physician-aided suicide, the "rights" of the fetus, and so forth.

The rhetor needs to consider that, Declaration of Independence or not, rights are established by convention, which convention originates in an ASSERTION that *X is* a right. The Equal Rights Amendment, we should remember, was a proposal that was *not* ratified by a sufficient number of states for it to become part of the Constitution. Legally speaking, women are thus not specifically constitutionally guaranteed the same rights as are guaranteed to men.

The claim to a "right," is, however, powerful within democracies, as is the reverse assertion that "You have no right to _____ " in the defense of a supposed individual freedom. As the Declaration illustrates, however, a claim to a right must finally be supported by law (local, national, or international) or by an appeal to the divine. To say that one should have *X* right, in other words, is quite different from saying that one actually has that right.

ROGERIAN ARGUMENT   (ROW *JAIR* EE UHN)
Rogerian argument is a concept borrowed by rhetoricians from the work of the psychologist Carl Rogers on non-threatening communication. It is closely related to all the complexities of ACCOMMODATION. Essentially Rogers argues that communications that *begin* with assertions are likely to immediately encounter hearer (reader) resistance. In place of the usual structure taught in composition classes of thesis, support, conclusion, the Rogerian argument substitutes question, alternatives, consideration of

alternatives, tentative conclusion based on alternatives examined. From the point of view of analytic rhetoric, the term *Rogerian argument* is thus descriptive rather than prescriptive. One does not, in other words, simply say, "This is a Rogerian argument, and it is therefore effective." See EFFECTIVE.

RULES

In court proceedings (on which the Toulmin models for argument are built, see WARRANT) and in DEBATE, there are rules and judges. Argument has no rules, and outside of the effect on the target audience, no judges. Language itself has no rules other than those that linguists try to derive from it by examination of its practice and, by the same token, no judges. This is not to say, of course, that there are not conventions. Nor is it to say that there are not styles of "acceptable" and "unacceptable" writing, provided that one observes at all times that "acceptability" always involves the question of "to whom." Because there are no rules does not mean that there are no negative consequences for not following the conventions. Consider:

> In constructing a sentence, never begin with a preposition or employ an absolute.
> Never use absolutes.
> No sentence fragments.
> The passive voice is not to be used.

See PRESCRIPTIVE.

SARCASM

It is questionable that sarcasm exists at all in *written* communication. If it does it could be described as exaggerated IRONY with DIALECT, or EYE DIALECT, or a typographical device (see TYPOGRAPHY) thrown in. Consider, for instance, a speaker saying "right" and saying the word over one second or over three seconds. Add inflection or dialect pronunciation to this, and you should have some idea of the complexity of conveying the same attitude with the same word *in print*. The analyst of written rhetoric is advised to reserve the word *sarcasm* for a description of speech and to use the word *irony* for written material. See IRONY.

SATIRE, SATIRICAL

Satire is a manner of ridicule employing extended IRONY in a presentation in which the reader is intended to recognize a correspondence to or parallel with a real-world occurrence, person, ideology, and so forth. It typically employs fantasy or exaggeration as a means of avoiding a direct representation of whatever is being satirized. What is vital to satire at its most intense is that the reader is offered some sort of a way into it, some way of recognizing that it is satire rather than the creation of a person with novel or unusual views.

To give some indication of the problems involved, consider how often you have heard, or read, *X* says of *Y* statement to *Z* person, "That's ridiculous." If the maker of Y statement *intends* for it to be ridiculous, she might thank *X*. If she does not, she is likely to ask what makes *X* think so or just say something like, "Not to me." My point here is that the "ridiculousness" of any given statement is often subject to argument and, more importantly, subject to argument for which there is no final arbiter, no final judge who can say, "Yes. You are right. It *really is* ridiculous." The problem the ironist consistently encounters is also present for the satirist, in that she can never be sure her irony or satire is understood *as* irony or *as* satire.

Take as example Swift's "A Modest Proposal" (probably the single most reprinted and well-known piece of satire in the language) in which the speaker proposes selling one-year-old Irish children as a meat product to provide the Irish poor with some source of income. If we did not know that this was written by Jonathan Swift and that he is noted as an Irish patriot *and* a satirist, there are only a limited number of points in the essay at which we can notice that it is satire: where, after having said that he doesn't want to hear of other solutions, he lists a number of them at some length and in italics; and where he shows the consumption of the children as meat to be a metaphor with his reference to the English in the antepenultimate paragraph ("For this kind of commodity will not bear exportation, the flesh being of too tender a consistency to admit a long continuance in salt, *although perhaps I could name a country which would be glad to eat up our whole nation without it.*" [my italics]).

In a period when grain that could prevent human starvation in Africa is routinely used to fatten feed-lot cattle used to produce sirloin steaks, filet mignon, fast-food burgers, and dog food, and when there is serious discussion of raising human clones as perfect-match organ transplant sources, one can hardly say that treating the children of the poor as a meat product, rather than letting them and others starve to death, is "ridiculous." See IRONY.

SAYING

The invocation of a "saying" is a type of ARGUMENT FROM AUTHORITY that assumes that the target audience is favorably disposed toward the body of information the saying represents. "Saying" is often considered the overall term for a group of words used to describe brief expressions taken to present wisdom, among which are ADAGE, APHORISM, epigram, FOLK SAYING, maxim, proverb, and saw (usually in the form of "old saw"). Be careful about assuming that what is introduced by "You know what they say" is venerable, however. Consider "You can't be too thin or too rich," which is not only recent but also, as any reformed anorexic can testify, wrong.

SCAPEGOAT

Scapegoat is so important rhetorically that a word that began as a noun is now a verb. Further, what began as a story of magical transference authorized by the God of the Old Testament (Leviticus, chapter 16, verses 21 and 22) has become a blameworthy and illegitimate act. To scapegoat is to find a single source to blame for whatever is the source of the complaint. Thus to blame inner-city blacks for the crime rate, television for violence, and recreational drug use for the threat to suburban America is to "scapegoat." See DEMONIZE, which is related but differs insofar as scapegoating does not need to involve the reconstruction of the other (see FEAR, APPEAL TO).

SCIENCE, ARGUMENT FROM

What I refer to as the "argument from science" is *not* the invocation of evidence gathered by scientists to support, adjust, or cast doubt upon a previous hypothesis. The argument from science is rather one of what I have called "authorizing" tropes (see TROPE). The "troping," in this case, is treating the vast and variously performed theater of inquiry traditionally called science as a single or monolithic enterprise that leads to the discovery of truth. An example would be "For many years there was no explanation for why objects fell until science proved the cause was gravity." The rhetorician should be conscious of such troping and of the subset of it called "research," which is often invoked in the same way (i.e., "research has proved . . ?").

SELF-EVIDENT

"We hold these truths to be self-evident . . ." may be the most famous occurrence of this term in English. In this usage, moreover, the term may escape the classification of BEGGING THE QUESTION to which terms like *obvious, speaks for itself, clear, undeniable,* and *indisputable* are subject, as are their negative forms *unbelievable, ridiculous, silly,* and, in its old meaning, *incredible.*

The passage from the Declaration may escape this via the insistence manifested in the phrase "We hold these truths." That is, the authors say to the British, from whom they are declaring their independence, not that the "truths" *are* self-evident, but rather that the group with which the British will have to deal will accept no argument to the contrary, will behave, in other words *as if* the "truths" were in fact (which nothing is) self-evident.

The "*Harper's* Index" and the various "quotes without comment" sections of newspapers and magazines count on the implicit attitude that those things cited "speak for themselves." Consider, however, that to make these citations so "speak" they have to be isolated from their original contexts and, in the case of the "*Harper's* Index," juxtaposed with other items. The following are from the September 1998 "*Harper's* Index":

Average annual amount the U.S. will spend on nuclear-arms programs through the year 2008: $4,500,000,000
Average annual U.S. spending on nuclear-arms programs during the Cold War: $3,700,000,000
Year by which Dan Quayle says he's convinced that Republicans "will select a nominee that will beat Bill Clinton": 2000

SEMANTICS

In rhetoric, *semantics* refers to the meanings of words. Hence no rhetorician would say, "That's just a question of semantics," which implies that the accused is merely quibbling over details rather than admitting that we all "really" know what is meant, that it doesn't matter what we "call" something as long as we all know what we are talking about. The rhetorician would hold to the contrary that what we call something is of vital importance to how we value it and would finally deny that a rose "by any other name would smell as sweet." See also EUPHEMISM and DEFINITION.

SET

Set is a formal term for a group or collection, the members (or member) of which possess specified characteristics. To return to the CLASSICAL SYLLOGISM, the PREMISE "All men are mortal" would be rendered as "All members of the set *'Homo sapiens'* are members of the set 'beings that die.'" "Socrates is a man" would be rendered as "All members of the set 'Socrates' are members of the set *'Homo sapiens.'*" The conclusion "Therefore Socrates is mortal" would be rendered as "Therefore all members of the set 'Socrates' are members of the set 'beings that die.'"

SEXIST LANGUAGE

Technically, sexist language is language that implies or asserts inequality based on gender. In current use, what is referred to as sexist language is usually language that is insensitive or offensive to those who are committed to social equality for women and is characterized by what those concerned would classify as inappropriate overt or covert gender differentiation. Like metaphor, gender differentiation can be found wherever one looks, depending, of course, on the breadth of one's sensitivity and/or definition (or, on whose ox is being gored). This parenthesis can serve as example. An ox is a castrated bovine above the age of five (before which age the bovine, if castrated, is a steer). The expression "whose ox is being gored" thus carries unmistakable gender overtones that would, unless the use of the phrase was ironic, make it unsuitable for the sentence in which I used it. In the original form of the entry for SOPHISTRY, I used the term "whipping boy" instead of the current "foil." At first blush, this is overtly sexist—it would seem that the sexism-sensitized writer should have either not used the phrase or used "whipping person" (in that "person" is not gender identifiable). Indeed, were it historically accurate, one should rather use "whipping child" because the reference seems to be to a youth who is beaten for the infractions of his or her owner or employer. Historically, however, the reference is specifically to a *boy* raised with a prince (male) or noble*man*, who is whipped for the misdeeds of the latter. The use in "freshman" has come down to us from Middle English as supposedly genderless, but considering that women then did not attend institutions of learning, one need not be impressed by such claims. I hear, with some frequency, supposedly educated and sensitive persons describing the act of complaining as "ragging" (as in "I don't know why he's been ragging on me about that; I wasn't even there when it happened"). That the speaker refers to a "he" makes it unlikely that the term's origins in the vulgarism "on the rag" (being in a menstrual period and hence hormonally disposed to irritability) are being invoked.

The matter of sexist terminology is complex and in a turmoil of historical change. The reader will no doubt have noticed that in this glossary I use the feminine pronoun in places where the masculine pronoun would traditionally be expected. Indeed, if the reader has not noticed, then the rhetorical strategy I am employing has not succeeded. My hope was that the first few times the reader noticed it she (or he) would be either pleased or annoyed at the implied social agenda (a kind of "affirmative action" for the feminine pronoun) but that after encountering it multiple times he or she would get so used to it that it would no longer distract him or her from the information material in the glossary entries.

My *final* hope for the strategy was (is) that the reader, after encountering the feminine pronoun continuously over many pages, would come to the conclusion that the use of "she" and "her" is as arbitrary as the use of "he" and "his," and as limiting. An editor for one of this text's earlier drafts wrote a number of unflattering comments in reference to the glossary's entry for *rhetoric,* among which was "Is this 'she' the same loathsome female who *claims* to be a graduating senior [see BEGGING THE QUESTION]?" The editor had refrained from commenting on the use of the feminine pronoun early on in the glossary in examples in which the person referred to was criticized, but here a sexist generalization (women and science don't mix) was suspected. Such was certainly not my intention, but my intention *was* that the consistent use of the feminine would bring the reader to the conclusion that it would make no sense to use the feminine pronoun rather than the masculine if it was used only when positive points were being made. The same applies if the behavior being described is currently associated with males but for no reason of anatomical necessity (see the baseball example in the entry for SPIN).

SEXIST LANGUAGE, AVOIDANCE OF

At the turn of the century, sexism still constitutes the norm in spoken and written English. Part of this, as mentioned in the previous entry, derives from its being built into the language itself. There is, as yet, no singular pronoun in English outside of *it* that is not gender identified, and the constructs *he/she* and *s/he* are nowhere near to having gained the social acceptability that *Ms (Ms.)* has (although the *he/she* construction seems to be gaining some ground in very short pieces of writing). What is unquestionably becoming more frequent is *they* with a singular antecedent. For instance, "When a writer begins an essay they sometimes find that the words come very easily." This example also involves the use of the plural verb "find" instead of the "finds" that the singular noun "writer" would call for. The form is now so common in spoken English that it is seldom noticed. It has not yet reached that level of acceptability in writing, however.

The use of nonsexist language will, in other words, call attention to itself and, depending on the audience and its relationship to the writer (is the writer a friend, a peer, a concerned citizen, a teacher, an "authority" of one kind or another, etc.?), will be registered as an aspect of that writer's politics and social agenda that will to some degree reinforce or interfere with the assimilation of the writer's thesis. Similarly, however, the use of blatantly sexist language will also be registered as an aspect, if not of the writer's social and political agenda, at least of their social and political "status" or "condition." (Did you notice the "their" in the previous sentence? If you did, I suggest that ten years from now you won't.) What constitutes blatantly sexist language? It depends. In the English department, we would search for a new chair. Another department might search for a new chairman (who, nevertheless, could be either a man or a woman). "NRA members and their wives are invited to . . ." would probably be seen as sexist by female NRA members, but it would create less of a stir than a similar reference to "IBM executives and their wives." "A giant leap for mankind" apparently didn't disturb anyone at NASA. The question here is not *is it* sexist, but rather is it *blatantly* sexist. Then it wasn't. Now, I suggest, "humanity" or "humankind" would be more likely than "mankind."

I hope I have here indicated that the matter is complex and too large for a document of this size to be fair to. I strongly recommend to all writers (and readers) Miller and Swift's *The Handbook of Nonsexist Writing,* at 180 pages in its second edition. In general the writer who wishes to avoid sexist language should be aware of gendered pronouns, traditionally male job descriptives that carry a gender tag (*mailman*), male references to groups (*Englishmen* when *the English* are meant), and titles that ostentatiously observe the gender of the referent (*madam chairwoman*).

SIMILE
A simile is a METAPHOR introduced by *like* or *as.*

SINCERITY
There is an apocryphal story of a famous newscaster who explained his success by attributing it to sincerity. "Sincerity is everything," he is reported to have said. "Once you learn to fake that, the rest is easy." In rhetorical consideration "sincerity" is a tonal aspect of the writer's *ethos.* Like "authenticity," it is something that is impossible to achieve as soon as one attempts it. If, in other words, I *try* to *be* sincere I cannot (although I may very well be able to *sound* sincere). As a rhetor what I can do is to try to *sound* sincere. Similarly, I can try to sound "authentic," but, of course, it is an effect aimed at rather than a state of consciousness. When a speaker overtly claims sincerity ("and I am being completely sincere now"), she usually does not

consider that the alert analyst might at that point ask, "Am I then to assume that up to this point you were being facetious, or perhaps ironic?" Most auditors and readers are not, however, attentive rhetorical analysts, so the claim will continue to be made, typically as a request to the reader to pay special attention to whatever statement follows. Frequently used claims to special consideration include "in all honesty," "to tell you the truth," "frankly," "to be completely candid," and the conspiratorial appeal to our vanity, "just between you and me."

SLANG

Slang used without the formal acknowledgment that it *is* slang (that is, without enclosing it in quotation marks) is characteristic of colloquial diction. Slang is, by definition, language that can be distinguished from STANDARD (educated) ENGLISH and indeed relies on the reader recognizing that distinction for its effect. Slang, hence, is the more or less private means of communication within a particular group (it is the "argot" of that group). Because of its eccentricity, expressiveness, vividness, ability to describe "new" ideas and attitudes, and often its precision, slang will frequently spread beyond the originating group into a kind of intermediate stage where it will be widely understood but still not accepted as a part of so-called STANDARD ENGLISH. When a word or expression has reached this stage, it is conventional to use it with no further acknowledgment of its status than enclosing it in quotation marks. At this stage the word or phrase is still considered slang. Having entered this stage (although the originating group may maintain it), slang is either assimilated by the language (and hence ceases to be slang), or it dies (in which case the user of "dead" slang is typically seen as hopelessly out of date). Slang in its primary stage (the private language of a group), when used in formal writing, will carry with it an explanation. Slang used in formal writing in its intermediary stage is usually enclosed in quotation marks. See JARGON.

SLIPPERY SLOPE

Slippery slope is a mode of argument in which the writer suggests that the proposed course of action or thinking being examined involves a principle that, if one commits oneself by assent to the proposed action or thinking, will lead to ultimate disaster. Like most other kinds of argument, slippery slope can be well or poorly handled. The argument that letting women attend universities would have the ultimate consequence of the destruction of college football as we know it is a slippery slope argument (and considering Title 9 legislation can no longer be considered far-fetched). So also is the argument that if we refused to discriminate on the basis of species we would ultimately be morally committed to starvation. The NRA continually lobbies against federal firearm regulation on the basis of a slippery slope argument ("If we let them forbid private ownership of assault rifles, sooner or later they'll come after our single-shot target pistols"). Or, "If we allow gays to serve openly in the military, it's just a matter of time until they'll demand lace curtains in the barracks." I would hope it is clear that to describe an argument as a slippery slope argument is not therefore to imply that it is well or poorly handled.

SLOGAN

A kind of motto, a slogan is intended to express an essential feature of the group with whom it is associated. It is usually short and simple, and it frequently contains words with powerful emotional associations: "Live Free or Die," "Don't Tread on Me," "Just Say No," "Don't Mess with Texas." In its brevity and intensity, it is intended to serve as a unifying device for the group that adopts it. See SOUND BITE.

SO-CALLED

Like quotation marks, the term *so-called* is frequently used to create a distance between the writer and a word she is employing. She will use a word because others use it, but she expresses her reservations concerning whether that word is precise or appropriate with "so-called" as a qualifying term. "So-called" can also be used as an introduction to a direct disagreement. "This so-called 'argument' is, in the final analysis, nothing but a direct attempt at intimidation." In this case the quotation marks are used to designate the word under discussion, but they could also be used as follows: "This 'argument,' in fact, is simple intimidation." The analyst should thus be careful to notice if the quotation marks indicate a word under discussion, the presentation of the words of another, or the fact that the writer is distancing herself from association with the word in quotes.

SOCIAL CONSTRUCTION, CONSTRUCTIONIST

The strict "social constructionist" insists that most, if not all, of those things that are thought to proceed from "nature" or that are "genetic" proceed instead from social attitudes that are (for the most part) linguistically conveyed. If, for instance, I find same-sex erotic attraction biologically explicable (thus "natural," see NATURE, ARGUMENT FROM), I am not, on that issue in any case, a social constructionist. The situation, however, is not so simple that one can say that either one is a social constructionist or that one is a BIOLOGICAL DETERMINIST. The distinction between these positions is vexed and, at the least, confused. This is so especially in terms of how one is to correct the situation one objects to. If I say that violence is to be attributed to movies, I am at a disadvantage in explaining the Inquisition or the treatment of Native Americans by the federal government. If I find homosexuality an indication of the decay of morals (and thus socially constructed), I am at a disadvantage in explaining male-to-male attraction as the norm in ancient Greece. The rhetorical analyst needs to be able to recognize that when an argument is postulated on either a biological determinist position or a social constructionist position, neither is "acceptable" outside of the consideration of those who comprise the target audience and what they are willing to accept.

SOCRATIC METHOD   (SEW *KRAT* ICK)
(Note: the relation of the term to the method used by Socrates as he is represented in Plato's dialogues is indirect. Like the term *Platonic love*, which has little to nothing to do with Plato, the *Socratic method* has come to have a life of its own.)

What is usually referred to when someone talks about this method is the behavior of a teacher who asks her students lots of questions instead of lecturing. To say thus that a teacher uses the Socratic method almost always is intended as praise (the student is "actively involved" in the "learning process," the classroom is a "collaboration," etc.). The reader who is interested only in what is usually intended by the term should stop reading here.

A former student of mine who became a teacher (and is now a college president) less enthusiastically referred to it as the "Guess what I'm thinking" method of classroom management, in which the student is rewarded, not for learning, but rather for playing the game of figuring out what the instructor has in mind. Our concern with it here is its appearance in written argument where my former student's characterization of the approach is particularly valuable.

The method takes two basic forms. The first of these most closely resembles the method represented as Socrates' and is briefly discussed under the entry for IRONY as "Socratic irony." Its purpose is not to establish a position as much as it is to destroy one. The reader, if she agreed with the position destroyed in the dialogue, is left in uncertainty and is thus presumably more susceptible to an (apparently) more satisfactory position, were it to be presented. The irony involved is the pretense on the part of the protagonist to not holding any position, to being herself uncertain at the outset, and indeed at the conclusion. She knows not *what* to think, but at least knows that one of the positions is *not* acceptable. It is this form of the argument, of course, that gives rise to the famous statement (attributed to Socrates by Plato) "He alone is wise who knows he knows nothing." This portion is the *elenchus,* or the "refutation." It holds, essentially, that uncertainty is preferable to error and flies directly in the face of the notion that if one has nothing positive to say one ought to say nothing.

In the method's second form (which is the best known and most commonly referred to by the term), the protagonist asks questions that lead the interlocutor to the recognition of a truth, which truth the interlocutor discovers within herself. An implicit part of the idea is that the individual questioned already knows the answer and would eventually (if so motivated) be able to arrive at it (discover it) unaided. The questioner only makes the process more efficient. The "teacher," within the system, is viewed as a facilitator for the discovery of knowledge rather than an imparter/provider of knowledge per se.

In its combined form, when the systematic destruction of certainty in a given idea or set of ideas is followed by the presentation of ideas that are supposedly inherent and thus "true," the method closely resembles what we have come to call, in a translation from Chinese, BRAINWASHING.

For this discussion, the key word is *lead*. The term *LEADING QUESTION* within our everyday vocabulary indicates something of the considerations appropriate in dealing with written representations of the method of argument. Two circumstances currently being treated as newsworthy constitute examples of what results from a "leading" question, or at least the arena in which the discussion is taking place: (1) "recovered memory" therapy and (2) police interrogations resulting in confessions (especially interrogations of "children" and/or minorities). There is considerable evidence in both of these areas to indicate that people can be brought to remember things that have never happened (indeed, it turns out, could not have happened). In the case of "recovered memory" therapy, psychiatric practitioners have gone so far as to state that patients are encouraged to exercise their imaginations and to speculate on what they *would* have felt if certain events *had* occurred (that they had been sexually abused as children, for instance).

Further complicating the matter is the necessity of questions to "beg," or assume, some aspect of the subject, which necessarily, even unavoidably, narrows the range of possible answers. You are probably familiar with this problem in relation to the use of "surveys" to ascertain "public opinion" in relation to whatever the sponsor of the survey is trying to find out. If, with Socrates, I ask a question like "What is the nature of truth?" I assume, with the question, that such a thing exists, I beg, as it were, the question of its existence in a more subtle but similar way to what I would be doing if I asked someone if she had stopped lying, or if I asked why it is that a given group is lazy. For the sake of clarity, take the exaggerated example of the sales representative trying to sell a two hundred-dollar smoke alarm asking, "What could be more important than your life? What could be more important than the lives of your children? Wouldn't you rather know that you had the best than to put their lives at risk?" Among the questions that are being begged here are: does a two hundred-dollar smoke alarm work better than a twelve-dollar smoke alarm? Can *not* buying a warning device be considered putting something at risk? Is the relationship between two hundred dollars and the value of life at issue—are there, in other words, other things that could be done with two hundred dollars that would make one's life, and the life of one's children, more valuable? Or consider, for another of the same type of example, a salesperson saying, "If I told you that this appliance could save you eight hundred dollars a year, even at current energy costs, would that interest you?" The salesperson is counting on your *not* saying. "*Are* you telling me that? Do you have data to support that figure? What would it cost me to 'save' that much, if that much were in fact to be saved?" Briefly, the question "What is the nature of truth?" assumes that truth exists, a conception that Nietzsche has demonstrated is not self-evident. See TRUTH.

A central reason, I suggest, that the Socratic method is typically seen as a mode of teaching rather than a mode of argument, and especially not a mode of "written" argument, is that its characteristic administration is through dialogue. Writing, in contrast, is frequently seen as a monologue. We are led to believe that the reclining or peripatetic philosopher conversed with his compatriots while another took notes and later published the record they constituted as a form of the original dialogue. Ostensibly the purpose of the publication is to lead the reader (who lacks the opportunity to hang out with Socrates, or whoever is the protagonist) to the same conclusion that the questioned came to (especially because the assumption is that there is only one correct answer and that it is the same for all people).

Among the problems to be specifically associated with the written forms are the following: (1) the narration of the dialogue, taking, as it must, the form of anecdote, is not dependable as an accurate rendition of what only may have happened (see ANECDOTE, ARGUMENT FROM) and can thus be "rigged" to take advantage of the target audience's areas of ignorance; (2) the method demands, without calling attention to it, acceptance of an epistemology that, were it made explicit, would raise objections from many; and (3) the method treats the questions themselves as if they were neutral, or "transparent."

Interesting as well is that a large part of the appeal of the method may involve the psychology of the reading audience's relation to the interlocutor. What is finally important, after all, is not that the interlocuter cleaned up her act and assumed the path of the virtuous, rather it is that the reader, the *witness* to the proceedings at a second remove, discovers the proper answer. We need to remember that the members of Socrates' audience in "The Apology" voted twice to execute him even after his argument that he should be sentenced to be supported by the state for the rest of his life. In response to the written form of the presentation of an argument by the Socratic method, the reader is given the option to side with the questioner while simultaneously identifying with the person being questioned. The questioner and the questioned are, finally, fictions (whether they have historically identifiable names or not), and audience response will inevitably be affected by the narrator's skills in presenting those individuals. That is to say, if I am Plato, and I am writing an argument, the rhetorical presentation of which involves a person named Socrates and an interlocutor named Meno (which Platonic dialogue of the same name, along with the "Euthyphro," the reader is urged to read), I will do my best to make Socrates witty and supply the reader, through Socrates' questions, information on which to base a poor opinion of the character (and intelligence) of Meno. By so doing I provide my audience members with the opportunity, if they shared Meno's opinions at the outset of the dialogue, to observe that these opinions are those of an ignorant and immoral person and are opposed by another person of great wit and integrity (Socrates). I have attempted thus to cause a relatively painless conversion (after all, she never even has to say she *used* to agree with Meno) on the reader's part from her former opinions to those that the dialogue supports not with logic, but with psychology. That Meno cannot defend his position–and the reader (who is not even asked to) may not be able to, either–does not amount to a demonstration that the position held is indefensible, or even inferior to whatever may be presented as a substitute for it.

SOPHISTRY   (*SAHF* ISS TREE)

Sophistry is usually understood as an illegitimate use of language to persuade. More generally the word is used to describe judging devices for their potential EFFECTIVENESS without consideration of their legitimacy. The sophist is, in this consideration, understood as being interested in winning the argument rather than being interested in its "correctness," soundness, or "truth." One of the goals of training in the branch of analytic rhetoric often referred to as "critical thinking" is to enable the trained to avoid being convinced by sophistry so understood.

There are arguments to the point that the self-called sophists were misrepresented by Socrates in order to use them as foils for his absolutist philosophy. One can know this, and know that it is arguably accurate, and still use the term *sophist* as indicated earlier. Bear in mind, however, that the word *sophisticated,* understood as beyond *naive,* derives from the same Greek term.

SORITES   (SUH *RYE* TEASE)

A sorites is a series of linked syllogisms in which the predicate term becomes the subject term of the following statement until the predicate is finally linked with the subject term of the original proposition. The following is a sorites. "Politics is the art of compromise, but compromise always yields less than was originally sought, which less, in the case of the matter of human survival, means not to survive, or at best not to survive for very long. In the face of inevitable death then it should be abundantly clear that nuclear disarmament is no subject to trust to politicians, or to consider as 'politically' soluble."

SOUND   (ADJECTIVE)

An argument or rhetorical position is held to be "sound" when (1) it is not fallacious, (2) it is valid, and (3) the premises from which it is derived are acceptable to "reasonable" persons. Obviously this last characteristic is problematic. It assumes, as indeed rhetorical theory in general does, agreement among a community using a particular form of discourse as to what is acceptable as "reasonable" or not. What is "reasonable" to a body of people whose members accept special revelation (direct communication from a deity to an individual), for example, will

not be accepted as such within a community of "human-
ists." Hence to pronounce any argument sound implicitly
invokes the given values of a community.

SOUND   (NOUN)

Alliteration is the repetition of initial sounds, as in Little
Orphan Annie's "leapin' lizards." In its simplest use it is intended to make the alliterated expression stand out from
words not so selected as a sort of mnemonic device, an aid
to memory. Along with assonance (the repetition or subtle
variation of vowel sounds) and consonance (the repetition
of either initial or terminal sounds, but usually terminal),
such word use is usually intended to invoke a sort of physically pleasurable response and to set up an anticipation of
development of the device. Rap music is an example of how
this is often intended to work. The expectation is that psy-
chologically and kinetically we are pleased by patterns and
by developing controlled variations within the patterns.
Thus the writer who can set up the anticipation of the next
phrase in her readers has her audience *participating in*
rather than judging or evaluating the rhetorical event. The
audience members, if this is successful, become not skepti-
cal targets (see TARGET AUDIENCE), but rather cocreators
who enter into (and are thus not resisting) the development
of the thesis. Part and parcel (alliteration) of sound is
rhythm, and the two (which can't be separated—"leapin'
lizards" has rhythm as well as sound repetition) make up
the qualities of language use that are often referred to as
"poetic" or "musical." Highly "figured" (see FIGURE OF
SPEECH) or "ornamented" language that emphasizes sound
and rhythm is often seen as appropriate for ceremonial occasions such as funerals, weddings, state speeches, or com-
memorative events. King's "I Have a Dream" speech at the
Lincoln Memorial is a classic example. How and why

sound and rhythm in spoken language as well as in written are found to be pleasing is a subject that currently lies outside of close definition but certainly relates to why the most seemingly banal song lyrics can have such large rhetorical effect. For instance, the success of the phrase in the song of the same name, "I can't get no satisfaction," defies conventional rhetorical explanation, but, like any anthem, is unarguably rhetorically significant.

As the reference to King's "I Have a Dream" speech shows, sound is most often thought of as a characteristic of the spoken rather than the written word. The song lyric I quoted, further, is *sung* rather than written *or* spoken. But we hear sound from the written word nevertheless, and we don't have to move our lips when we read to do it. To read the "Gettysburg Address" cut into the marble on the left hand of the seated statue of Lincoln at his Washington memorial is inescapably to "hear" it, despite the fact that, unlike King's speech, there are no recordings. So also is our experience with poetry, which we "hear" from the printed page, frequently with no conception of what the voice of the poet sounds like.

SOUND BITE

The term *sound bite* may pick up some cachet from its computer lingo sound-alikes, *byte* and *bit*. More operatively, however, it relies on the comparison to how much one can "bite off" at one time, what constitutes, thus, a "mouthful" by this measure. These bites, nevertheless, come in two sizes, what I think of as motto or bumpersticker length as opposed to inspirational or contemplative length. In theory the idea of the "bite" developed from the news media's approach to excerpting speeches for the so-called "ten o'clock news." What was sought was something catchy and characteristic that could be used to represent the larger message that time constraints would not allow to be included. What happened was that speechwriters—and now, given the brief cite boxes (in the trade a "pull-quote" or "raised quote") characteristic of periodical presentation of longer prose pieces, prose writers—began to compose for the brief memorable cite. These teasers, as it were, not only add visual interest to the page but also encourage the reader to continue through the ordinary prose for the sake of the catchy phrase that she will encounter if she does.

Historically, sound bites probably derive from war cries or "host shouts," rallying cries intended to reinforce the solidarity of the clan or "host" (Wallace's "FREEDOM," from Gibson's *Braveheart* or "Remember the Alamo"), and they still carry the same characteristics. They are formulaic, memorable, brief, and typically have some sort of sound or syntax manipulation that raises them above ordinary speech (see SLOGAN).

The sound bite can be very powerful if it succeeds in establishing itself in the public memory, or in the memory of the controlling group. Johnny Cochran's "If the glove don't fit, you must acquit" from the Simpson trial is recently memorable, and JFK's "Ask not . . ." formulation survives as a sort of odd legacy. It can be argued that "Hey, hey, LBJ, how many kids did you kill today?," "Make love, not war," and "Hell, no, we won't go" directly influenced the conduct of the Vietnam War and/or resulted in Lyndon Johnson not standing for a second term.

Consider the following bumper-sticker-length sound bites in terms of their dual function to solidify supporters and publicly define a position. Note that humor is a frequent component.

Custer Died for Your Sins
A Woman without a Man Is Like a Fish without a Bicycle
Kill 'em All, and Let God Sort 'em Out
No More Nukes
Nuke the Gay Whales
What If They Gave a War and No One Came?

SPIN

Presumably the term *spin* derives from billiards and then baseball. A billiard player will put "backspin" on the cue ball by striking it below center with the intention of preventing it from following the object ball into the pocket. A pitcher, similarly, will attempt to influence the direction the ball will travel off the bat, or how it will behave in the air between the time it leaves her hand and the time, if the calculation and execution are correct, it encounters either the bat or the catcher's mitt. To spin something thus is to attempt to influence its *reception* in a particular direction or with a particular emphasis. Politically, a "spin doctor" is a person who "interprets" a speech or a document for the media in a light favorable to the position being represented. Spin is roughly equivalent to interpretation, so to spin is to interpret, to say what conclusion, from the point of view of your camp, should be drawn from a particular set of data. See TAKE.

STANDARD ENGLISH

Standard English refers to the grammar and syntax that are held to be acceptable by users of the language who consider themselves educated. As such it is a PRESCRIPTIVE rather than a descriptive term that implies that the person who does or can use Standard English is more knowledgeable than one who does or cannot. It implies thus that English not considered "standard" is therefore "substandard." Standard English is sometimes considered a DIALECT, but it can be argued that it was created precisely not to have the characteristics of dialect–that is to say, that it is not to be identified with a region. See EDUCATED USAGE.

STASIS
Stasis comes to us from classical rhetoric as a name for the possible "issues" with which the rhetor could deal. The number of these differs according to the rhetorician consulted. The list I present here follows Lanham. The possible issues can concern: (1) "fact," (2) "definition," (3) "value," (4) "number," and (5) "jurisdiction" or, as Lanham presents them, "conjectural, definitive, qualitative, quantitative, relative." The categories, regardless of how many there "really" are, offer an interesting grid within which to find an answer to the question "What is really being argued here?," an answer to which can be very useful in terms of selecting rhetorical strategies relevant to a particular target audience.

STATISTICS
Benjamin Disraeli, prime minister to Queen Victoria, is reputed to be the source of the tripartite division of the category "lies" into "lies, damned lies, and statistics." It appears as well in Mark Twain's *Autobiography*. At their best, statistics can be offered in *support* of an argument, but, like "facts," they *prove* nothing. A statistical correlation is taken (by statisticians) to indicate, according to its strength, a high or low *probability* of a causal relationship. The term *statistically significant* has the technical meaning that the probability that a given event is due to chance alone is one in twenty or more. Further, a statistical correlation presumes that *all other factors are held equal*, which, from the

use of the word *all*, simple inspection will show to be impossible (although, certainly, one can do one's best). The rhetorician must consider that all statistics have sources, that they are all compiled by one or another group and from one or another instrument. Each of these factors complicates the conclusions that can, even tentatively, be drawn from their results. We can suspect that, for instance, when the tobacco industry says that there is no *proven* link between smoking and lung cancer, members are relying on this characteristic of statistical information and that in their own studies they are looking for a particular sort of evidence (that which will support their position).

A recent issue of the *Harvard Heart Letter* reported a study of data on 4,500 people who had been evaluated regularly over a period of thirty-five years that showed that when the population was divided into four groups according to height, there was a higher risk of heart attack in the shortest group (a fifty-one percent increase in risk of dying and a forty-two percent risk of dying from heart disease). This would seem to indicate that "shortness" relates to an increased risk. However, when the data were adjusted for age, much of the difference disappeared. The average age of the men in the shortest group, for example, was 4.5 years higher than the average age of the members of the tallest group. Combining this with the continuing tendency of younger people to be taller, increased complicating risks in an older population, and the fact that beginning at about age forty people gradually lose height due to bone and joint changes indicated that it was unlikely that "shortness" was in itself a predictive or causative factor. The key idea here is to remember the assumption involved in *all other factors being equal.*

Consider, moreover, that it is statistically accurate that the *average* American has *very slightly* less than one testicle. Consider as well (in the light of the T-shirt slogan "When all else fails, manipulate the data") the difficulties involved in *disputing* someone else's data, in demonstrating either that they are erroneous (i.e., that mistakes were made) or falsified (i.e., that fraud was perpetrated). Statistics remain, however, a very powerful source of support for an argument. The basic modes of replying to them are (1) offering another and differing set of statistics, (2) offering a competing factor (like "age" in the preceding example), or (3) denying that the data lead to the conclusions claimed to be drawn from them by offering an alternative conclusion that could be reached from the same data.

STRAW MAN
A "straw man" argument is one that attributes a position to the opposition that the opposition does not hold or claim and then proceeds to attack that position instead of the real one. The "straw man" is a dummy, in other words, and not the "real" man (position) who is ostensibly attacked.

SUBJECTIVE
See OBJECTIVE. Subjectivity is inevitable. It is, however, recognized as a virtue both to admit it and to avoid generalizing on the basis of it. Hence the statement "Soccer is boring" is not *only* subjective but also borders on the stupid (like "'Heavy metal' is just noise"). What the rhetorician hears in a statement like "Soccer is boring" (the rhetorician recognizing that the word *boring* refers to an inescapably subjective view) is "I have not developed the sensibility necessary to appreciate soccer and [probably] resent discussion of it, which forces me to face that deficiency." So, "objectively" speaking, *is* soccer boring? Rhetorically considered, this is a nonquestion. One could reply only, "Boring to whom?" When we complain, then,

of a "lack of objectivity" in some report, we are not complaining about the *presence* of subjectivity (which is inevitable), we are instead complaining about the lack of *more than one viewpoint*. Instead of *one* subjectivity, or subjective view, we are asking for a number of them. The entry at OBJECTIVE presents a hierarchy of words that purports to indicate locations on a supposed range of possible positions between subjectivity (as one endpoint) and objectivity (as the other). See EITHER/OR.

SUMMARY

Summary would hardly seem to need a rhetorical definition, but it constitutes, along with the "synopsis" and the "abstract" (especially if that is written by a person other than the original author of the material being "abstracted"), one of the most subtle methods of argument. In Rogerian therapy (see ROGERIAN ARGUMENT), each of the participants is required to summarize what the other has said *in terms that are acceptable to the person being summarized*. In the usual conditions in which we find summary, no such conditions are enforced. No therapist is present. The reader, in other words, is likely to accept a summary on the basis that it is plausible rather than that it is accurate. Indeed, were the target audience familiar with the position being summarized, the summary would be unnecessary. It is thus to be expected that the summary presented will be put in a way the writer finds most advantageous to her position. Hence, rhetorically, all summaries are suspect.

SURD

A surd is any unproven point that is accepted as a *beginning* proposition in an argument. If a participant in the argument objects to the beginning proposition, it ceases to be a surd, and the logical process moves backward until a proposition is found upon which the participants can agree. For instance, in the argument that concludes "Socrates is mortal," the major premise "All men are mortal" is a surd (see discussion under PROOF). If someone objects to the proposition because it is unprovable, she might be asked if, *admitting* that it is unprovable, she was willing to accept the proposition provisionally for the purposes of the argument. We often encounter the idea of a surd in the word *given,* as in a statement like "Given that sea turtles are endangered. . . ." See especially here FAITH and BELIEF. These terms are so intimately related that it can be argued that the term *surd* has been employed for no other reason than to avoid the term *belief* and its associations, *surd* being in some way more philosophically respectable.

SYLLOGISM   (*SILL* UH JISM)

The simplest way to think of a syllogism is as three statements, the last of which purports to derive its authority from assent to the previous two. A syllogism is a formal logical statement of an argument in the form of two premises from which a third statement (the conclusion) is held to follow. They exist in three basic forms and combinations. Aristotelian logic deals with categorical syllogisms (those based on the relations among sets) and the possible forms of these that are held to be valid, all formed of some of the possible combinations of the four types of categorical premises (see PREMISE). Another form is the HYPOTHETICAL SYLLOGISM, a construction such as:

If *A*, then *B*.
A.
Therefore *B*.

The construction of the DISJUNCTIVE SYLLOGISM, takes the form:

> Either *A* or *B*.
> Not *B*.
> Therefore *A*.

(See also ENTHYMEME.) An argument is not in itself a syllogism until it is reduced to or translated into these formal logical constructions.

SYMPATHY, CLAIM OF

Bill Clinton's "I feel your pain," ridiculed as it was as cheap and opportunistic, succeeded with the target audience as an invocation of emotional empathy. If I can convince you that I do indeed "feel your pain," then you are free to assume a number of things, among which are that (1) you are not beneath me or apart from me to an extent that forbids my understanding and sympathy, (2) I am a person with a depth of feeling similar to your own, (3) I acknowledge in my own being your right to your feelings.

SYNECDOCHE   (SIN *NECK* DUH KEY)

Synecdoche refers to a powerful and often-used set of FIGURES OF SPEECH that can subtly or not so subtly load a referent negatively or positively. The various forms are (1) a part for the whole ("crown" for king, "redneck" for a rustic); (2) the whole for a part ("the government" for a particular administration, "the administration" for a president); (3) the specific for the general ("hired gun" for an assassin, "ambulance chaser" for a lawyer); (4) the general for the specific ("criminal" for an embezzler, "soldier" for a paratrooper); and even (5) the material for the thing made of it (a jockey's "silks," a police officer's "iron"). The use of synecdoche can appear to be a clever or witty variation from the mundane and everyday, but bear in mind that NAMING, which synecdoche is, is among the most powerful means of making indirect value judgments. To refer to a group of women as "ladies" (part for the whole—only some women are or would wish to be considered "ladies," no matter how that term is defined) is to assert that the group as a whole is, or even ought to be, whatever the term connotes. One could also argue that to refer to a group of human females as "women" rather than as "people" constitutes synecdoche (part for the whole) as surely as does referring to members of either gender by a slang term for their genitalia. *Synecdoche* is now generally taken to be synonymous with *metonymy* and is used in preference to it. More importantly, like metaphor, synecdoche is one of the subcategories of the group of figures referred to as TROPES, the importance of which to argument can hardly be overemphasized. See NAMING.

TABULA RASA   (*TOB* YOU LAH *RAS* UH)

The term *tabula rasa* is usually translated from the Latin as "blank slate" (although "erased tablet" is closer). It refers to a theory of the content (or lack thereof) of the mind at birth and is most closely associated with the late seventeenth-century English philosopher John Locke. We are probably most familiar with the concept in relation to the so-called "nature versus nurture" argument, the central question of which is to what extent we are shaped by environment (nurture) and to what extent we are "born" whatever way we are (nature). The blank slate idea argues, of course, that we are written upon by experience and are so wholly shaped by that.

The concepts involved are extremely important as epistemological tropes and crop up in differing forms throughout the history of Western thought. Plato's DOCTRINE OF

RECOLLECTION, for instance, is a variation on, or perhaps the point of origin for, the "nature" argument.

In terms of argument about responsibility (and much argument is about responsibility), the nurture argument comes down on the side of rehabilitation, whereas the nature argument supports permanent incarceration or execution. The idea of incarceration as punishment from which the incarcerated will learn her lesson is, of course, an argument from nurture. The rhetorical analyst would be well advised to attempt to come to some sort of position concerning the subject writer's position within this problematic.

TACT

A descriptive, but not very informative, definition of *tact* calls it the art of making a point without making an enemy. As there is no assured way to convince, there is no assured way to avoid giving offense. But, insofar as the reasons for taking offense are even less rational than those for which we change our views, some psychological postulates can be advanced. The writer-reader relationship is a great deal less risky in terms of giving offense than is the speaker-auditor relationship. In a speaking situation, for instance, ridicule will offend with fair consistency (unless, of course, the "audience" is comprised of volunteers who came to one whose stock-in-trade is insult and ridicule [plug in the name of your favorite stand-up comedian]). There are a number of vital differences here between a reader and an auditor:

1) The reader is alone. Not even the writer is "present." Only the text is present, and the text is totally nonjudgmental. In the case of satire, for instance, the reader can be the "object" of the satire and nevertheless be able to find her former position "ridiculous." No one is there to

laugh at her. There is no one there for whom a show of indignation need be put on.

2)   The reader has time. The reader can put the text down, go have some light refreshment, mow the lawn, chat with her neighbors, mention what she has been reading to *X,* and return to the text (or not) at whatever time suits her.

3)   The reader has space. Recognizing that space cannot be separated in any final way from time, the spatial relationship with the physical presence of a text still differs radically from the spatial relationship between an auditor and a speaker. A reader, unlike an auditor, can go back and read the first paragraph again, or can skip to the end. The reader can, in the presence of the text, rethink, reconsider.

4)   The reader can react without social inhibition (unless she is in a library or the like). Unlike an auditor, the reader can say "bullshit" *and* throw the argument against the wall. Then, given item 3, if the reader feels better after doing that, which is likely, she can pick the text up again, and the text doesn't mind. This may sound facetious, but it is seriously advanced. Most of those elements that inhibit, or limit, an auditor's response, whether the situation is face-to-face or the auditor is a member of an audience, are absent in the writer-reader relationship.

This is not to say that the reader *will* do these things, but it is to say that the reader *can* do these things. Given the preceding, what then can be said about the writerly exercise of tact? Target audience is of primary consideration:

1)   If the writer seeks alliance with a group that defines itself by what, or who, it rejects, tactful behavior toward the rejected, unless clearly ironic, is not likely to be appreciated.

2) If, however, the audience is comprised of those who are being attacked by the argument, and the approach is ridicule, then the writer (remembering that, after all, she has time) should do her best to insure that the ridicule is funny, so funny that the object of the ridicule will have to grin. After all, none of her friends can see her do so. She can do it safely. And then maybe think, "Well, that *is* ridiculous."

3) If the target audience is comprised of the uncommitted, the demands on the writer remain much the same. The uncommitted would like to think of themselves as fair, so ridicule is not a good idea. The uncommitted would also like to think that they are capable of deciding among competing positions, and, if they recognize them, they are likely to be offended by rhetorical devices that assume their ignorance or lack of sophistication.

One hopes, at this stage, that the reader would laugh any attempt to set down rules off the page. Clearly, given the various natures of various target audiences, it makes no sense to say, "Write an argument that you would not find offensive." What can be said, however, is, "Write an argument that to the best of your judgment will be convincing to those you wish to convince."

TAKE   (NOUN)
See OBJECTIVE. This term points up an aspect of the notion of *spin*, to the effect that it does not permit the idea of a "neutral," or unspun, "reading," "position," or "viewpoint." The rhetorical analyst will notice that each of these latter terms is compromised by the implicit admission that it does not refer to *the* "reading," "position," or "viewpoint" and cannot, consequently, be considered as neutral. When a person is asked what her "take" is on an incident, it is

implied that *any* response constitutes *a* take. Presumably the term comes from film argot (specifically, the way a particular section of film is identified on a clapboard as "take 1," "take 2," etc.), probably combined with the sense of the word as we would use it in the expression "When you told her, how did she *take* it?"

TARGET AUDIENCE

See WARRANT and EITHER/OR. The target audience is the audience a given writer in a particular piece of work wishes to convince of her thesis. The concept is complicated by several considerations: concerning the thesis, is the thesis type overt, implied, and/or covert?; concerning degrees of persuasion, does the writer wish to produce doubt, toleration, acceptance, conversion, general or specific action?; and concerning a time frame, is the writer pursuing an immediate reaction, establishing a position for the record, or laying a foundation for future development?

Take, as an example of a subject area, questions concerning the civil rights of homosexuals. Let us say that writer A holds the position that homosexuals are entitled to the same civil protections as heterosexuals–that is to say that a homosexual should have legal protection against discrimination on the basis of sexual orientation and practice identical to that of a heterosexual. Let us further say that writer A defines her target audience as all those who are undecided on the question and the range of those who oppose her position. This is a simple and straightforward designation. Still, it is more complex than a mere EITHER/OR designation would permit (either you are in favor of this, or you are opposed to it).

In the following diagram labeled "target audience continuum," I have tried to represent the range of possible positions in relation to this (and, abstractly, any other) particular position on a definable subject. At the extreme right (assignment as right or left here is completely arbitrary; it could as well be reversed) is the person or persons who not only agree but also are willing to devote their lives working to obtain these rights and ensuring in militant and even violent action that those rights are observed. To the left of this group are people who agree and are willing to contribute time and money to the cause, but not their lives; and to their left, people who agree and would vote to support such legislation but who would not contribute money or time; and to their left, people who agree in "principle" but would rather the subject not be discussed. (These are very rough distinctions, and I hope the reader understands they are not meant to be exhaustive but rather to illustrate the idea of "degrees" of commitment.) I represent this in the diagram by moving from black at the far right through lighter and lighter grays as we move toward the undecided area.

In the center of the diagram are two fields (shown as connected *between* the pro and con continuums with dotted lines). The (arbitrarily) top range, labeled "undecided," is composed of those who have not made up their minds concerning their position. People in this undecided group find themselves sympathetic or unsympathetic to varying degrees but would not act to express that sympathy or lack of it. Those on the right of the classification are *inclined* in the pro direction, but not committed to it. The proximity of this undecided position to the weakest of the pro positions is indicated by only a slightly less dense gray than in the left end of the pro section. To their left is a white area defining a "middle" or neutral group, followed by increasingly dense grays intended to designate the undecided group that is suspicious of the idea and hence inclined in the con direction, but (as with the other extreme of the undecided category) that would not act to express that position.

Below that group (and parallel to it) is the range I designate as the "what?" group. The population of this group occupies the same position between the pro and con continuums but is not *even* undecided. Members of this group are not familiar with the question–do not know there *is* a question. The right and the left of the "what?" group, indicated by an increasing density of grays in each direction, each has a *little* information about the subject, but that information comes predominantly from the nearer of either the pro or the con position.

To the left of these two groups is the continuum of con positions, ranging from those who are opposed but would rather not talk about it and would not act, to the extreme group that would advocate, say, violent public extermination of homosexuals as infectious "sexual deviants." Bear in mind that in this last category I am describing an extreme. That such a position is likely to be described as insane is consistent with my point in terms of defining that extreme. So also with the right extreme of the continuum. That degree of concern could be considered obsessive, and finally unbalanced.

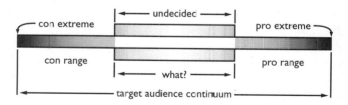

The group that I designated as the target audience in my "basic" example–that is, all those people who are undecided about their position with respect to her position and the range of those who oppose her position–includes *everyone* to the left of the pro range. Initially this might seem like a simple and sensible division, but the characteristics of the selected group are so varied that it is unlikely, on the face of it, that the right extreme of the undecided range would respond positively to being classified with the extreme left (those at the boundary of the con classification). Such a target audience is possible, but not likely given the limited number of arguments that would appeal to *all* members of this hypothesized "target" group. After consideration, it is much more likely that writer A will decide to make no attempt to appeal to the extreme, and indeed may choose even to compliment the now-smaller targeted group of those opposed on *not* being members of the extreme (the "crazies").

The principle that I am trying to establish here is that a skilled writer will compose her arguments with a specific range of readers in mind and that any notion of the EFFECTIVENESS of the argument must take into consideration what that audience will be willing to WARRANT. Arguments do not exist in a void. Rather, they are all located in a historical place/time–they are in *a* language and presented at *a* time, and consequent on that, addressed not to *all* readers/speakers of the language, but rather to the particular subgroup that will warrant the arguments' central assumptions.

For the rhetorician, then, there is no such thing as a "general audience." In practice such a designation would mean that no *particular* audience is being addressed and hence that the "question" of audience has no apparent relevance to the rhetoric of the essay in question. That such a situation could exist is dubious. From the perspective of the analyst (rather than the producer) of argument, Toulmin's concept of the WARRANT provides an excellent tool for identifying the intended or target audience. If, for example, the rhetorical analyst encounters the statement "God did not intend for us to 'tolerate' homosexuals, and He says so very clearly in the Bible . . . ," she can be fairly confident that the essay is addressed to people who accept the Bible as the word of God and who are not, or at least don't think they are, homosexuals. This is the group that would warrant such a statement. In any case, the identity of the target audience must be derived from the essay itself, and one of the most efficient means available is a process of elimination (i.e., the analyst initially determines what particular groups are *not* part of it). External evidence such as place of publication, date of publication, and medium (remember that a number of newspapers condemned the "Gettysburg Address" as a failure *as a speech*) is useful, but never definitive.

Writer A, then, may choose to whom to pitch her argument from among the entire range. She might choose the far right side of the cons and the whole range of the "what?" group. Alternatively she may direct her argument only to the members of the undecided group, and so forth. She may, if her aim is to produce action, pitch her argument to the left side of the pro group in an effort to move them into the group that will vote for the subject position. Or she may pitch her argument to the far right of the pro group in an effort to have its members suspend their activity during some time of crucial opinion gathering.

This moves us into a further complication related to what I referred to as "degrees of persuasion" at the beginning of this discussion. It may be writer A's goal to move people from the right range of the opposed into the range of the undecided, and to that end writer A may pose questions intended not to convince the opposed that she is right, but rather to introduce doubt about the rightness of opposition. We are given to the either/or sort of thinking that leads to the idea that those who are not our friends and allies are therefore our enemies. If, however, by the introduction of doubt I can prevent a group from aiding my enemy, my cause is advanced. Let us say a vote was to be taken. Prior to the presentation of B's argument, eight were for the position, seven did not want to get involved, and eight were opposed. If B's argument is constructed in such a way that it can move *one* person from the opposed into the group that does not want to get involved, B's side wins the vote. In other words, to affect *change* with an argument one does not need to make converts. One needs only to introduce sufficient doubt to keep the weakest of the opposition from participating in opposing the argument (like *not* going to the polls).

From this perspective, some arguments are designed to drive people away from a position, others to attract people to a position, and still others to induce those who already hold an agreeing position to take some specific action.

Finally we come to the time consideration. U.S. Supreme Court justices who have voted with the minority often write a dissenting opinion. Why? They have, after all, lost the argument—they have been unable to convince a sufficient number of their fellow justices of the correctness of their position. I suggest that they do so because they recognize that court decisions never take place outside of particular political and historical circumstances (the place/time I mentioned earlier) and that these circumstances, inevitably, change. Consequently, what is a losing position today may turn out to be a winning position in the future. The argument, if you will, is not written to convince now, but rather to become an item of record to solidify the position of its supporters toward that time in the future when the circumstances will allow another perspective, and in this particular application, when the membership of the court changes.

TASTE, ARGUMENT FROM

Although it may seem an odd entry as a rhetorical term, the *argument from taste* is one of the earliest examples of what has now come to be labeled "cultural relativism," albeit presented, usually, on a micro (individual) rather than a macro (culture) scale. The central concept is expressed in a number of commonplaces: "To each his own," "There's no disputing taste," "I don't know anything about X [wine, food, beer, art, music, etc.] but I know what I like," *"Chacun a son gout"* (which, used by someone writing in English, adds a sort of double appeal to authority in that the French are notorious "connoisseurs" of things "fine" [fashion, wine, "cuisine"], so when *they* say "each to his own taste" they *must* know what they are talking about), "Beauty is in the eye of the beholder," "Whatever turns you on" (or the interesting obverse, "Whatever gets you off"), "Different strokes for different folks," "Whatever floats your boat," and so forth.

At issue, in the long run, is the question of whether there can be, say, a "beautiful" landscape on the dark side of Jupiter. When an object, "natural" or not, is described as "beautiful," the analyst should ask herself if this is meant as an ABSOLUTE judgment (i.e., simply put, if you disagree you are wrong) or if it is offered as an "educated" opinion in which, indirectly, the reader is invited to compare her degree of "education" with that of the writer and decide if perhaps she might be missing out on recognizing the quality of something because of her inability to appreciate it.

We have a number of expressions that incorporate this latter attitude, which implies that taste is "learned" and that tastes are hierarchical, depending on the quality of the "education" from which the particular taste is learned. I overheard, for instance, in a recent discussion of the qualities of various brands of gin, "That's an acquired taste–I have an American palate."

TAUTOLOGY
A statement that is tautological is circular (see BEGGING THE QUESTION). It is true *by definition* and as such differs from truth statements about the world around. The statement "A coward is a person who lacks courage" is tautological to the extent that "cowardice" *is defined* as "being without courage." So-called "right-to-life" proponents would hold that the statement "Abortion is murder" is, *by definition,* indisputable, that is, that the statement is a tautology ("murder" being here defined as the taking of life without consent). So-called "pro-choice" advocates would deny that the statement is a tautology by not assenting to the implied definition of "life." An interesting tautological commonplace is the invocation of the Darwinian "survival of the fittest." Those who survive are, *by definition,* "the fittest." See NAMING and DEFINITION.

TELEOLOGICAL ARGUMENT, THE
Teleology is the study of purpose in the natural world or history. It is a kind of associative carryover from our ability to make things that help us to solve problems. If I want to crack a nut, for instance, I turn a rock into a hammer. When I attach that rock to a handle and use it to drive nails, I have created an object with a particular purpose. I may then make a leap to the assumption that things that I have not made have a "purpose," are "for" something, as the hammer is for the expansion of my ability to deal with other matter (nuts, wood, sheet metal, stone, whatever).

Once I have begun this process of investing the world with purpose I can make all sorts of wonderful assignments. I can, for instance, assume that the "purpose" of the females of species is to bear young and thus that anything that might interfere with the "fulfillment" of that purpose is "unnatural" (see NATURE, ARGUMENT FROM) or even evil, and consequently justify bombing abortion clinics on the basis of teleology.

The teleological argument at some point or another becomes part and parcel of the argument from design, which, quite simply, assumes that everything that *is* must have been *made* (i.e., it must have come from somewhere for some reason) and that therefore there must be a maker for those things that *we* did not make (rocks, trees, animals, etc.) and further that the maker made these things for a purpose, whether we are aware of that purpose or not.

It would be difficult to overestimate the importance and prevalence of applications of this argument. It is used, for instance, to support the sanctity of the "family" and to define that construct; it is used to identify the "role" of women; it underpins theories of the superiority of one or another "race"; and, in combination with revelation, it is used to define the superiority of one or another religion. That's just for starters.

The rhetorical analyst should be particularly alert for claims concerning the "nature" of the subject of the argument and how these relate to claims about its purpose.

TENTATIVENESS

Although it is often urged upon writers that "strong" writing give the appearance of confidence and that she who wishes to convince others must appear to be convinced herself, all the principles standing behind conceptions of ROGERIAN ARGUMENT argue that this is only sometimes accurate and, again, dependent on the nature of the relationship the writer wishes to establish with the reader. The tentativeness of the Rogerian is that what is offered as a solution to a problem is offered as the result of the best information the writer possesses at the time, on the basis of what looks best among the available positions. Such an approach can be attractive because the reader may be brought to see the writer as looking for the "best" solution as opposed to simply pushing people to accept "her" solution. Thus "Maybe it won't work, but can we *try* this?" is often more attractive than "If you were smart [implied, 'like I am'], this is what you would do."

TEXT

In the loosest definition, a text is anything that can be "read" if we understand the term *read* to mean "interpret." From the perspective of the rhetorician, the text is that fixed hard copy that constitutes the subject to be investigated–if we want to resolve a question about the rhetoric of a given piece, we go to the text on the assumption that the text has primacy over what a given writer might say a text says, or what she intended for a text to say.

This seemingly straightforward designation becomes problematic, however, as soon as any kind of editorial process is encountered and, as is the case with a great deal of print argument, the original piece has been edited for length, or language, or the policy of the particular place of publication. A syndicated column, for instance, that appears in one newspaper may appear in another without three of its original paragraphs and with a totally different title. The copy editor is likely to have made a space decision based on what else was being placed on the page. For this reason we need to be sure that in a given discussion we are all talking about the same iteration or version of a given text, the original version of which may be simply unavailable or become available only when the writer puts together a collection of such columns, in which process she would *usually* work from her original file rather than whatever edited form had appeared in a given newspaper.

Some of the implications of this from the perspective of the analyst are that it cannot be presumed that if a column appears in the *New York Times* that it was written for whatever audience it is assumed regularly reads that paper. The same column (or a length- and title-edited version of it) may very well be appearing at the same time in the *Washington Post* and the *San Francisco Examiner.*

There is a further difficulty when, as we must, we involve the historical setting of a text in combination with the question of original intention. An immediately available example is the famous "We hold these truths to be self-evident, that all men are created equal; that they are endowed by their Creator with certain unalienable Rights, that among these are Life, Liberty, and the pursuit of Happiness." Lincoln argued that Jefferson and the founding fathers could write and pass this language despite the fact that many of them were, and continued to be, slaveholders, not because, as many historians would argue. they did not see black Africans as "men," but rather because they saw the statement as one that was simultaneously true in principle and false in "fact," as it was and had been administered in the world. He argued thus that the Declaration constitutes the ideal; the Constitution, the practical. The Constitution can be changed, the Declaration cannot. Changes in the Constitution, then, should be in the direction of bringing it into accord with the Declaration.

Let us then leave this definition of *text* with the following qualification. Insofar as it is possible to determine, the text is that item of writing *considered in its most formal aspect,* that is, as an *accurate* reproduction of the original print iteration. The reader will thus realize that what has been cited earlier from the Declaration of Independence is not the text for the simple reason that it is an excerpt, a selection, from that document, and in that it is a selection, the selection inescapably constitutes an interpretation.

THESIS

The thesis of an essay is its point; it is the position that the writer wishes the TARGET AUDIENCE to accept as a result of the argument; it is the answer to the question that created the occasion for the argument in the first place. Simple as this may seem, however, determination of precisely what the thesis of a given piece of writing is can be highly problematic. Real-world rhetoric, unlike the argument papers frequently produced in composition or rhetoric classes, often leaves the thesis unstated and often fronts one thesis while only implying another and perhaps more important one.

We may consider theses as being of three types: overt, implicit, and covert. In this taxonomy the latter two classifications are not mutually exclusive. The implied thesis is not stated as a thesis–most often it must be constructed from the WARRANTS and implications of the argument. The covert thesis is implied as well, but it is, moreover, hidden or disguised. The rhetorical analyst will be able to distinguish the overt from the implied and covert thesis immediately in that the overt thesis will be, as its name suggests, open and observable. The implied or covert thesis, on the other hand, will often need to be argued for and evidence presented from the text to establish it as a thesis. The distinction between implicit and covert theses is one of degree. The presence of an implicit thesis can be argued even though it is nowhere directly stated in the essay in question. The covert thesis, however, must be inferred, usually at a much more subtle level. Garry Wills, in his *Lincoln at Gettysburg,* argues that the effect on the Constitution of Lincoln's 1863 address

> altered the document from within, by appeal from its letter to the spirit, subtly changing the recalcitrant stuff of that legal compromise, bringing it to its own indictment. By *implicitly* [italics mine] doing this, he [Lincoln] performed one of the most daring acts of open-air sleight-of-hand ever witnessed by the unsuspecting. Everyone in that vast throng of thousands was having his or her intellectual pocket picked. The crowd departed with a new thing in its ideological luggage, that new constitution Lincoln had substituted for the one they brought there with them.

Wills is referring, of course, to the *explicit* acceptance of slavery by the Constitution and Lincoln's importation of the *implicit* "spirit" of the Declaration ("that all men are created equal"). Lincoln's *explicit* thesis is that the Union must be preserved ("that government of the people, by the people, and for the people shall not perish from the earth"). The *implicit* thesis is that the Union must be reborn, that "the cause" for which the soldiers buried at Gettysburg died was a *new* "birth of freedom" in which the "all men are created equal" of the Declaration is taken into the Constitution, which document physically incorporated it in 1865 with the Thirteenth Amendment.

Another example of the implicit thesis can be drawn from Judy Brady's much-reprinted "Why I Want a Wife." In that essay the writer indulges in an ironing-board reverie concerning what her desiderata would be were she to acquire a wife. The piece concludes with the following brief paragraphs.

. . . I want a wife who understands that my sexual needs
may entail more than strict adherence to monogamy. I must,
after all, be able to relate to people as fully as possible.

If, by chance, I find another person more suitable as a
wife than the wife I already have, I want the liberty to re-
place my present wife with another one. Naturally I will expect a fresh, new life; my wife will take the children and be
solely responsible for them so that I am left free.

When I am through with school and have a job, I want
my wife to quit working and remain at home so that my wife
can more fully and completely take care of a wife's duties.

My God, who *wouldn't* want a wife?

The overt thesis is that everyone should have a wife. This
implies, however, that the population from which these
wives will be drawn is other than "everyone" (as in the reputed construction "There wouldn't be any objection to
slavery if everybody had a slave") and so less than, or other
than, human. I would argue that Brady's *implicit* thesis is
that were the term "wife" stripped of its gender associations (as Brady's avoidance of gender-specific pronouns
throughout the essay implies) and treated simply as a non-
gender-specific job description, no one would apply. Why
this thesis is implicit rather than overt is (along with the
inescapable egotism of the persona of the fantasizing
would-be consumer) a central aspect of Brady's rhetorical
approach. As with satire in which the satirized is presented
with so much detail that she can avoid the defensive reaction typically attendant upon recognizing that one is being
attacked and see the object of the satire as ridiculous, the
implied thesis allows the object of the argument to con-
template the attack without taking it directly or personally.
She (or in this case, he) is made to look ridiculous but, (1)
no one but he notices, so he has time to correct his behavior and (2) he can recognize that although he *resembles* the
figure presented he is not "that bad."

The covert thesis is more difficult to illustrate without a full essay to draw from and is always arguable (see especially RHETORICAL ANALYSIS). Given that, two items from Gilbert Highet's rhetorical analysis of the "Gettysburg Address" may serve as an example (with the proviso, as always in analysis, that the reader may have a more satisfactory explanation of the details of Highet's presentation). Here is the beginning of Highet's fifth paragraph.

> There are many accounts of the day itself, 19 November 1863. There are many descriptions of Lincoln, all showing the same curious blend of grandeur and awkwardness, or lack of dignity, or—it would be best to call it humility. In the procession he rode horseback: a tall lean man in a high plug hat, straddling a short horse, with his feet too near the ground.

I would argue that Highet has gone a long way to produce a word that none of the eyewitness accounts uses—"humility." His claim in the presentation is that the eyewitnesses are all describing the same thing, except that none of them has the "right" word for it, the word that Highet can derive from reading the lot. His own approach, further, is masked in a kind of humility of its own, a tentativeness in which it is hoped the reader sees him groping toward and finally finding the "right" word that no one else could come up with. Five paragraphs later we encounter

> . . . the famous description of our State as "government of the people, by the people, for the people" was adumbrated by Daniel Webster in 1830 (he spoke of "the people's government, made for the people, and answerable to the people") and then elaborated in 1854 by the abolitionist Theodore Parker (as "government of all the people, by all of the people, for all the people").

Lincoln's speech was formulated in late 1863. Highet tells us that Daniel Webster, some thirty-three years earlier, presented an outline of, foreshadowed a line from that speech, and Parker, just nine years prior to the event, got the picture a little clearer. This is an amazing claim. Highet implies that the "Gettysburg Address" existed *as a future event* many years before it came to pass. Lincoln did not adapt his statement from these writers, rather they glimpsed, albeit imperfectly, *what he was going to say.* This, inescapably, is what "adumbrated" means here. Then I remember that Lincoln died, and the Union lived, and that another figure entered a town on a ceremonial occasion on a too-small animal, and that large among this figure's virtues was humility, and that he died for the salvation of his people.

Here, I suggest, is the derivation of and argument for a covert thesis, one that Highet did not wish to make directly—that Lincoln participated, at least, in divinity and that his sacrifice bears direct comparison to Christ's, that his words, like scripture, were prophesied, and that because of his sacrifice "we" (notice Highet's phrase "our State") shall not perish.

TONE

In rhetoric tone may be most understandable in comparison to what we refer to when we speak of "tone of voice" (as in, for instance, "Don't use that tone of voice with me"). Thus any word that could be used to describe tone of voice could be used to describe a rhetorical "tone." The obvious difference is that an essay has no "sound" (see SOUND, particularly the last paragraph); it is precisely in this *not* comparable to a speech. Thus in order to suggest this "sound," the writer is forced to the resources of diction and structure. It is important, however, not to confuse "tone" with "level of diction" (colloquial through poetic, for instance). Thus one's tone can be ironic (not SARCASTIC), gentle, pleading, impatient, condescending, formal, and so forth, but not educated, slangy, heightened, blue collar, or the like.

Complicating the matter is the association of tone with truth-telling and with the supposed "objective" stance. *Reportorial*, for instance, is a word that may be associated with *tone*. There are particular formulae that are associated with the reportorial, among which are use of the passive voice and whatever device will make the reporter a sort of invisible medium through which information passes on its way to the reader. Example: "Sources close to the X today indicated that the situation with Y is not as stable as has been presumed. One respondent, very close to Z, told this [newspaper, reporter, journal, inquirer, or even "reporter"] that the X is seriously considering q."

This, in itself, constitutes an argument, but more particularly we are here interested in the incorporation of this tone into argument that does not represent itself as reportage. Example: "There is a remarkable unanimity among researchers on this topic to the effect that early exposure to X behavior in circumstances that, for lack of a comparative base, could be taken as constituting a norm, is a strong predictor of Y in later life." Traditionally material that employs this tone is referred to as "reportage" rather than as "argument."

TRADITION, APPEAL TO

The appeal to tradition, or to "the past," is an aspect of the APPEAL TO FEAR in that what is projected as the "other" is here "change." Additionally, the tradition, or "past," that is appealed to is a construct that frequently did not exist, or if it did, existed for a very small number of people (consider, for instance, the "tradition" of the "Old South," which is frequently invoked, is from the perspective of the wealthy plantation owner, of whom there were relatively few). It is nevertheless a powerful argument frequently employed in relation to what we frequently think of as "the good old days, when _____." You fill in the blank. Some suggestions: "when people didn't have to lock their doors," "when you weren't taking your life in your hands just to walk down the street," "when kids used to say 'yes, sir' and 'yes, ma'am' and 'please' and 'thank you,'" "when a high school diploma meant you could read and write," "when people used to work for a living instead of just looking for a handout," "when comedians didn't feel like they had to use four-letter words to be funny," "when people believed in honesty and a day's work for a day's pay," "when if you acted like a lady you were treated like one," "when people like that knew their place."

What the rhetorical analyst needs to be sensitive to in such appeals is what past is invoked and what that past is intended to represent for the target audience (as distinctly opposed to those who just might happen across the piece of writing).

TROPE

A trope is a FIGURE OF SPEECH. The term is convenient not only because it is shorter than *figure of speech* but also because it can be used as a verb, as in, for instance, the statement "The writer tropes on the resemblance between 'red' and 'read.'" In classical rhetoric, tropes were held to be of four types: IRONY, METAPHOR, SYNECDOCHE, and *metonymy,* which latter is currently considered as synonymous with *synecdoche* and is so considered in this glossary.

As I hope the discussions of metaphor and synecdoche indicate, the concepts involved as these relate to how users of language name and categorize the world and their experiences in it are vital to analytic approaches to written argument. Kenneth Burke, among others, suggests that tropes and the process of "troping" constitute a, if not the, major way in which we organize our linguistic relationship to the world around. Burke designates irony, metonymy, metaphor, and synecdoche as "Master" tropes, by which I think he intends that they comprise the major divisions of the concept.

I have proposed another and hierarchical designation using what I refer to as "authorizing tropes," a designation that does not delineate a kind of trope but that instead identifies particular tropes as historically and socially privileged (i.e., given special "authority" in a given time and a given society). The concept allows the rhetorician a means to side-step the urge to evaluate while delineating how a given authorizing trope is being used. It is important that the reader understand that my designation of an argument as an authorizing trope says nothing about the "truth" of that argument. The rhetorician using the designation has the advantage of being able to discuss the particular application of the trope in a specific piece of writing without having to argue beliefs.

Those items discussed as authorizing tropes in this glossary are, alphabetically, HISTORY, LOGIC, NATURE, and SCIENCE and are referred to as (for instance) NATURE, ARGUMENT FROM, and so forth. The list could contain many more items (the teleological argument, for instance), and the reader is encouraged to argue with this selection in terms of major authorizing tropes that it omits. For the purposes of rhetoric, understanding what authorizing tropes are, understanding the principle involved in so designating a term, is much more important than agreeing to the content of any list of them.

TRUE
That statement that is in accord with known evidence and capable of being held by "reasonable" beings is said to be "true." Do not confuse this term with VALID. Other views would hold that the concept of "truth" is an authorizing trope (see TROPE) entailing the invocation of a static, and finally mystic, referential absolute. Rhetorically it is important to recognize a truth claim and that its reference is to a statement that is held as being in accord with "reality."

TRUISM
In nonanalytic usage a truism is a statement with which no one would argue–a "self-evident" truth. From the perspective of the rhetorical analyst, a truism, like a platitude, a cliché, or a commonplace, is a statement *presented as if it were self-evident* on the basis of its frequent invocation. That something has been said again and again is, we know, no reason to assume its accuracy. So, as with the cliché, to employ a truism is not necessarily to indicate a lack of original thought, but is in itself a rhetorical strategy. Many people are comfortable with clichés, which, indeed, is how such statements became clichés in the first place.

TRUTH
"Truth" is conformity to the actual. To determine it thus we must be acquainted with the "actual" at first hand. Nietzsche asserts that language, that aspect of rhetoric with which we are dealing here, is incapable of presenting the "actual" at first hand, but must instead resort to metaphor, the creation of a "figure" to stand for the reality that cannot be directly presented linguistically. Truth is thus, as one of Nietzsche's editors puts it, "a rhetorical construction arising from the creative use of language for the purpose of making an effective social arrangement." The translator for the following is

Daniel Breazeale. I remind the reader that because a statement is outrageous does not indicate that it is false.

> What then is truth? A movable host of metaphors, metonymies, and anthropomorphisms: in short, a sum of human relations which have been poetically and rhetorically intensified, transferred, and embellished and which, after long usage, seem to a people to be fixed, canonical, and binding. Truths are illusions which we have forgotten are illusions; they are metaphors that have become worn out and have been drained of sensuous force, coins which have lost their embossing and are now considered as metal and no longer as coins. . . . [T]o be truthful means to employ the usual metaphors. Thus, to express it morally, this is the duty to lie according to a fixed convention, to lie with the herd and in a manner binding upon everyone.

TRUTH CLAIMS

A truth claim may be explicit, as in "And we know it is true that in cases of X we always encounter Y" or less clearly made, as in "Although it has been claimed that in cases of X we always encounter Y, really what happens is Z." In the latter statement the truth claim lies in the word "really" used as a less assertive version of "the truth is, however, that," which could be put in its place. At a greater distance from the explicit claim is a statement like "Although many people think that in cases of X we always encounter Y, it is only Z." The following expressions could be inserted into the statement before "only" as emphasis, but they would not change the claim itself: *in fact, in reality, really, indeed, actually, without a doubt, certainly,* and so forth. It is important for the rhetorician to recognize when she or another is making a truth claim, as opposed to presenting a hypothesis, and further to recognize that such a claim is an assertion, not an argument. See GIVEN for a discussion of the hypothetical. A dispute involving competing truth claims often resembles the youthful "argument" "Is so," "Is not," "Is so," "Is *not.*"

TU QUOQUE   (TOO *KWO* QUAY; LATIN FOR "YOU'RE ANOTHER")
We see this in a number of forms, for instance: "Who are you to talk?," "Who doesn't?," "People in glass houses shouldn't throw stones," "Let he who is without sin cast the first stone," and so forth. The argument is intended to, and often does, silence the accuser. Typically the concept is used to affect a sort of *quid pro quo*, that is, if you stop talking about this, I won't talk about that.

TYPOGRAPHICAL DEVICES
Italics, capital letters, quotation marks, and boldface are often means to try to impart the emphasis to parts of a piece of writing that a speaker could convey with her voice. Odd spellings are also so used. The discussion of sarcasm mentions that the amount of time spent to *say* the word "right" can indicate that it is meant sarcastically. Irony can be indicated in a piece of writing by spelling that mimics that dragged-out pronunciation, such as "riiiight." Quotation marks are also frequently used to imply "so-called" and thus to express reservations about the use or meaning of the word so quoted. In the entry for the word *true*, for instance, note that the word *reasonable* is in quotes to signal "so-called," or even the ironic "whatever *that* might mean," which is typically meant to imply that on consideration "that" turns out to be meaningless. See also the e-mail icons discussed at the close of the entry for SARCASM.

UNDERSTATEMENT
Understatement is a form of irony, typically with the intention of calling attention to the importance of something by

obviously claiming less for it than would ordinarily be expected. *Litotes* (*lie* tuh tease), from Greek, is the name of a particular form of understatement in which the opposite of a value is negated. Rather than say, "It is vitally important that we realize that this could result in a nuclear war in which humanity may well be destroyed" we would say, "The possibility of this action resulting in nuclear war in which humanity may well be destroyed is not trivial." See MODESTY.

UNINTERESTED
Do not confuse the statements "I am *uninterested* in X," which means that X bores me, and "I am *disinterested* concerning X," which means that how the issue of X is resolved will neither benefit nor harm me. I have no "interest" (stake, stock, investment, involved relatives or family members) in it.

UNIVERSAL AFFIRMATIVE
See PREMISE. The universal affirmative is a statement that takes the form "All *A* is *B*," that is, all members of the set A are members of the set B.

UNIVERSAL NEGATIVE
See PREMISE. The universal negative is a statement that takes the form "No *A* is *B*," that is, no member of the set A is a member of the set B.

UR
When two items resemble each other but have no known area of contact, an "ur" source is sometimes postulated as an explanation for the similarity. An ur argument would be the hypothetical (i.e., undiscovered) source of two similar arguments. See the final paragraph in DICTIONARY, A.

VALID

The word *valid* is frequently used to mean "true." In rhetoric and logic, however, there is no necessary relationship between validity and truth. To state that an argument or syllogism is valid is to affirm that the rules of logic have been properly used in deriving the conclusion from a given set of premises. Consider the following: "All green things are basketballs. This is a green thing. Therefore this is a basketball." The argument is valid. The conclusion is properly drawn from the premises. The conclusion (*This* is a basketball), however, may or may not be true.

1) I stand before you with a basketball in my hand and say, "All green things are basketballs. This is a green thing. Therefore this is a basketball." The argument is valid. Both premises are false, but the conclusion is true—this *is* a basketball.

2) I stand before you with a lime in my hand and say, "All green things are basketballs. This is a green thing. Therefore this is a basketball." The argument is valid. The first premise is false, the second is true, and the conclusion is false—this is a lime, not a basketball.

3) I stand before you with a lemon in my hand and say, "All green things are basketballs. This is a green thing. Therefore this is a basketball." The argument is valid. Now, both premises are false, and again the conclusion is false—this is a lemon, not a basketball.

In each of these three cases *the form of the argument* is valid. To say thus that an argument is valid is to say that the rules of logic have been followed in its composition, *nothing more.* Any inquiry into the truth of a given conclusion depends on affirming as true the premises from which that conclusion is validly derived. Remember the following formulation: *validity is a property of arguments–not statements. Neither a statement nor a conclusion can be "valid." Only arguments admit of validity.* See INVALID and TRUE.

VERNACULAR

The vernacular is the language as it is spoken by "ordinary people" in "everyday life." In rhetoric as we are here considering it, *vernacular* would be used to describe language that is deliberately written to call to mind everyday speech. The "mother" of so-called literary usage, or educated usage, becomes, for instance, "mom" or "momma." Instead of writing to William Safire, "Surely, Mr. Safire, you cannot expect us to believe this . . ." we might write, "Aw, come on, Bill, give us a break, for crying out loud." If the writer uses the vernacular frequently (like Molly Ivins, for instance, or Mark Twain), it is usually meant to suggest an absence of pretension and a genuineness that is often associated with a "down home" manner of expression. Its apparent lack of sophistication is often presumed to reflect well on the integrity of the speaker ("make the speaker look good"). Like the "plain style" and "objectivity," however, each is a result of a deliberate rhetorical choice and so used for effect and is hence neither unsophisticated nor genuine (whatever that might mean).

The term *vernacular* is sometimes used as understatement to describe speech or writing that is viewed as socially inappropriate or obscene. "Ms. Clinton, at this point, invited her interlocutor to initiate osculation with her gluteus maximus. She did so, however, in the vernacular." See COLLOQUIAL.

VOICE

The frequency with which we use the word *voice* in talking about writing illustrates how closely we traditionally associate the two and how conditioned we are to hearing with what I have called "the mind's ear." To "give voice to" means to express, but more specifically it means to "put into words" the previously "unspoken." As frequently, however, we refer to a voice as an IDEOLECT. As technology has shown us, and as music lovers have always known, voice, in this sense, is unique, whether it belongs to a Stradivarius or a soprano. The writer has found her voice when her writing is recognizable and associated with whatever *ethos* she has been able to construct for herself. See *ETHOS* and TONE.

WARRANT

The most common rhetorical use of this term derives from its use by the contemporary philosopher Stephen Toulmin in his important *The Uses of Argument.* The term is used in a technical way in this glossary, but it has very similar conversational meaning. When the police wish to search a location, it is not uncommon for them to be asked if they have a warrant. A warrant, here, is "official permission." A warrant in terms of rhetoric is permission from an audience. We thus can say of a statement that it is warranted or unwarranted on the basis of its acceptability to a given audience. Discussion of this term is closely related to discussion of *assertion* and *fact.* What an audience is willing to accept provisionally as true, or accurate, can be considered as "warranted." If I say that fifty-two percent of *Homo sapiens* alive today are female, it is likely that after a bit of consideration a reader would say, "All right. And?" The reader would, in other words, accept the statement. It is thus "warranted."

Note, however, that what is warranted for one audience may not be warranted for another. What is warranted for one historical period is in another unwarranted. What is warranted for one philosophical or religious orientation is not warranted for another. If we want to think about the term again in terms of the original example, *it is the audience that grants the warrant.* No statement is warranted on its own. Thus it is inappropriate for the rhetorical analyst to say anything like "*X* statement is warranted because there can be no sound morality without a belief in a supreme being." *X* statement is or is not warranted *because a given audience would or would not accept it as such,* not because of some piece of external information that might be taken as corroborating whatever the claim of *X* is. If the rhetorical analyst finds that one or more of the assertions presented in a given argument appear to her to be unwarranted, it does not follow that the statements *are* unwarranted—it is more likely that she is not a member of the target audience. See TARGET AUDIENCE.

WE, THE EDITORIAL

It is publishing convention that editors or members of an editorial staff refer to themselves as "we," presumably to create the impression that the newspaper, magazine, or journal "speaks," as it were, with a single voice. Thus it is further the convention that such editorials are unsigned, which allows *The Nation* or the *Los Angeles Times* to "endorse" political candidates as if they were themselves thinking entities.

ZEUGMA   (ZOOG MUH)

To employ *zeugma* is to use different senses of the same word in similar grammatical constructions. Lying under oath and lying under the witness seem to be more closely related than some would like to admit.

GLOSSARY ENTRIES

A Scan List

■═══════■

Note: A parenthesis following an entry in the scan list indicates that discussion of that entry occurs in the entry corresponding to the content of the parenthesis. The glossary proper, for instance, does not contain an entry for ACTIVE VOICE. That term is, however, discussed in the entry for PASSIVE VOICE.

absolute
abstract, abstraction
academic argument
accident
accommodation
accommodators
acronym
active voice (*SEE* passive voice)
ad absurdum
ad baculum
ad feminam
ad hoc
ad hominem
ad hominem circumstantial
ad ignorantium (*SEE* ignorance, argument from)
ad misericordium
ad populum
ad vericundium (*SEE* authority, argument from)
adage (*SEE* aphorism)
affectation, affected
alliteration (*SEE* sound [noun])
allusion
ambiguity
analogy
analysis
anaphora

tradition, appeal to
trite (*SEE* cliché)
trope
true
truism
truth
truth claims
tu quoque
typographical devices

understatement
undistributed middle (*SEE*
    distribution)
uninterested

universal affirmative
universal negative
ur

valid
vernacular
voice

warrant
we, the editorial

you're another (*SEE tu quoque*)

zeugma